FLOP MUSICALS OF THE TWENTY-FIRST CENTURY

Flop Musicals of the Twenty-First Century offers a provocative and revealing historical narrative of a group of musicals that cost millions, that were created by world-renowned writers and directors, and that had spectacular potential... but bombed anyway.

Stephen Purdy asks the reader to consider what the legendary creators of *Les Misérables*, pop superstar Elton John, and wunderkind Julie Taymor have in common besides being inspired storytellers of iconic Broadway musicals. The answer is that they also all created shows that, for one reason or a dozen, flopped. This book shares the story of what can happen when formidable creative teams of sell-out musicals attempt to repeat their success but miss the mark. First-hand accounts from the cast members, backstage staff, and the creative team, combined with a wealth of secondary sources gathered from press articles, reviews, and critical commentary, offer an intriguing insight into the factors behind success and failure in the musical theatre business.

This is a fascinating book for students, scholars, practitioners, and fans of musical theatre that contains thoughtful observations about luck and creative differences, botched adaptations, and alienated audiences, all of which can determine the fate of a musical.

Stephen Purdy is a member of the musical theatre faculty at Marymount Manhattan College in New York City, USA, and is the author of *Musical Theatre Song: A Comprehensive Course*. He regularly delivers master classes and seminars on musical theatre singing and song performance at arts institutions across the globe.

FLOP MUSICALS OF THE TWENTY-FIRST CENTURY

How They Happened, When They Happened (And What We've Learned)

Stephen Purdy

Routledge
Taylor & Francis Group

LONDON AND NEW YORK

First published 2020
by Routledge
2 Park Square, Milton Park, Abingdon, Oxon OX14 4RN

and by Routledge
52 Vanderbilt Avenue, New York, NY 10017

Routledge is an imprint of the Taylor & Francis Group, an informa business

British Library Cataloguing-in-Publication Data
A catalogue record for this book is available from the British Library

Library of Congress Cataloging-in-Publication Data
Names: Purdy, Stephen, author.
Title: Flop musicals of the twenty-first century: how they happened, when they happened (and what we've learned) / Stephen Purdy.
Description: [1.] | New York: Taylor & Francis, 2020. |
Includes bibliographical references.
Identifiers: LCCN 2020003100 (print) | LCCN 2020003101 (ebook) |
ISBN 9780367173326 (paperback) | ISBN 9780367173319 (hardback) |
ISBN 9780429056222 (ebook)
Subjects: LCSH: Musicals–21st century–History and criticism.
Classification: LCC ML2054 .P87 2020 (print) |
LCC ML2054 (ebook) | DDC 792.609/05–dc23
LC record available at https://lccn.loc.gov/2020003100
LC ebook record available at https://lccn.loc.gov/2020003101

ISBN: 978-0-367-17331-9 (hbk)
ISBN: 978-0-367-17332-6 (pbk)
ISBN: 978-0-429-05622-2 (ebk)

Typeset in Bembo
by Newgen Publishing UK

CONTENTS

ACKNOWLEDGMENTS

Heartfelt thanks are extended to the members of the production teams and casts of the shows discussed in this volume who were exceedingly generous with their time and forthright with their responses. To a large extent, I have relied on those who were there to string the pieces of the stories of these shows together in order to provide a seamless narrative. Without them, the degree of continuity that I strived for from the outset would not have been possible.

I also thank the staff at Routledge for their always timely and unwavering support as this book came together, especially Ben Piggott, my indefatigable editor who encouraged me throughout the process.

Many thanks go as well to my academic family at Marymount Manhattan College in New York City, especially Patricia Hoag Simon, for the years of loyalty and inspiration.

Finally, thank you to my family—Kendall, Caden, Rowan, and Mom—for their patience and understanding while I wrote this book. I am more grateful than you will ever know.

INTRODUCTION

I suppose people cry at weddings because once you get beyond the spectacle of the thing you get to something along the lines of brazen optimism. The implacable union of souls standing there before us renews a certain conviction and hopefulness even in the most hard-hearted among us. Just imagine the possibilities.

The first day of rehearsal for any theatre production, musical or non, isn't altogether different. It's a giddy celebration of the artistic union of not two alone, but of many souls: Writers, directors, actors, designers, and support staff, all bountifully optimistic that this time it will all go just right. Just imagine the possibilities.

Sometimes from these beginnings the perfect alchemy of good fortune and great theatrical minds align and theatre voodoo works its wonders. And what a boon to live inside a hit. For all the rewrites, do-overs, ice packs, and hurry-up-to-waits, there are handsome returns.

But for other shows there lie hard times ahead. In the commercial theatre ethos, in particular, there may be a litany of reasons as to why. Quite often the show itself isn't particularly a good one. Weakness isn't well tolerated in the theatre, certainly not at extraordinarily high ticket prices, and weakness, no matter the strengths that may be at hand, may ring the death knell for the show sooner rather than later. Here in the Main Stem, only the strong survive as shows endeavor to find their audiences. Many shows struggle to capture a share of seat-fillers, not because the quality of the product isn't attractive but rather because the topical matter in the show isn't especially stimulating. Timing is often an unforgiving offender, too. World events can even spell an untimely demise for shows. Tourists staying home make for uneasy bottom lines in the theatre business. Changing tastes, too, may account for shows being placed in uncomfortable predicaments; even shows that are admirably crafted and stocked with entertainment value and winning content are sometimes shooed away by ticket buyers, even dismissed as passé as tastes and preferences shift.

There may also be economic factors in play: Less disposable income and ever-increasing ticket prices may mean that potential ticket buyers can become aroused by a "most bang for your buck" philosophy, preferring eye-candy shows to shows that may place emphasis on form over substance and craft.

But then there are the other shows. Sometimes a show, try hard as it may, just can't get it right and is an all-around stinker. You've seen a few, I've seen a few—those shows that confound common sense, weren't bright ideas for musicalizing, or were just abject misfires that evolved from a sincere idea that had a solid foundation but materialized quite differently than the original vision.

In short, there are many reasons why musicals fail but really only one—audiences stop coming. The musicals included in this volume represent a hearty cross section of all of the above. I register them here not as relics in a museum of oddities but rather because I believe the collection assembled here represents a fair illustration of the many reasons a musical can falter, from artistic to economic, from sour luck to sleepy subject matter. In choosing this group of musicals for the purpose of discussion in this volume, I considered many criteria, including the mistaken notion that, in order to be considered a flop, a musical must merely close quickly and not return on its investment or some portion of it. To the contrary, *Spider-Man: Turn Off the Dark* ran over a thousand performances but returned little of its capitalization to investors and was therefore defined as a "flop." Notwithstanding, since 2000 there have also been many shows that did close with brief runs and certainly before payoff. In narrowing that list, it was clear to see that a great number of these were steered by venerated, accomplished, and intelligent theatre artists. Like a sort of theatrical Moses, these guys and dolls seem to have the inside line to the man upstairs as to how to make a musical work, and when they miss it's a real head-scratcher as to why the shipwreck. But fail these musicals did, even with the mighty at the helm. I've seen firsthand a floundering show at the hands of brilliant people unable to resuscitate the patient, and it can be a doozy of a thing to witness. In placing the above two criteria at the front and center of the selection process, the musicals included here were chosen. But alas, due to space and time restraints all of the flop musicals that appeared on Broadway since 2000 cannot be represented here so if you're asking yourself "Hey, what happened to *Sweet Smell of Success* and *Doctor Zhivago*?," look for those in future volumes.

In this book, I don't intend to offer a wholesale take on how the shows could have been fixed. If the most astute minds of the theatre couldn't figure out how to have made these shows run on Broadway, then I certainly cannot. Instead, here I am keen to reveal what the ill-fortune of these shows may be able to teach us by discovering what went wrong along the way; discussing the merits of turning certain topical matter into musical; what the critical and audience responses were; what the responses were from those directly involved; and when, where, and how things might have begun to career out of control. To accomplish the most cogent narrative, I relied heavily on the remembrances of those who were there and endeavored to tell the most factually accurate stories possible. Memory is imperfect, however, and any factual misrepresentations will be corrected in future editions.

So let's take a front-row seat for some shows that, let's face it, had the best of intentions but didn't work or did work and despite that simply didn't find an audience, sometimes dying one of those protracted musical theatre deaths that is widely and highly publicized, creating messiness everywhere, crushing egos, and leaving behind a trunk load of folklore.

And I'm not above some dish every now and then.

Viva la musical theatre!

1

SPIDER-MAN: TURN OFF THE DARK

Opened June 14, 2011
Closed January 4, 2014

Never bite off more than you can reasonably chew.

Key dramatis personae

Julie Taymor, Director, Co-Book Writer: Celebrated film and theatre director
of *The Lion King* and others and MacArthur "Genius Grant" Fellowship
winner.
Glen Berger, Book Writer: Playwright and Emmy Award–winning writer.
The Edge, Music and Lyrics: Singer/Songwriter of the Irish Rock Band U2.
Bono, Music and Lyrics: Lead Guitarist/Songwriter of the Irish Rock Band U2.
Michael Cohl, Producer: Concert promoter and theatrical producer who
Fortune magazine once dubbed the "Howard Hughes of rock and roll."
David Garfinkle, Producer: Entertainment lawyer turned theatrical producer.
Marvel Comics, Owner of the Spider-Man "brand."
Philip William McKinley: Credited as "Creative Consultant" on *Spider-Man: Turn Off the Dark*.

Story-wise, *Spider-Man* is a shrill, insipid mess, a musical aimed squarely at
a Cub Scout demographic. Looking at the sad results you're compelled to
wonder: Where did all those tens of millions go?

Peter Marks, Washington Post, *February 7, 2011, on the*
occasion of the "fauxpening"

Spider-Man: Turn Off the Dark

It was the pervasive, running joke that Broadway season. And the unfunniest. Who would be the next casualty of the calamitous technical foul-ups over at the Foxwoods Theatre and would it be, God forbid, worse next time than the last? The New York theatre community was incensed. Late night television shows were spoofing the show with no letup. *New Yorker* magazine lampooned the show's misfortunes by running a cover cartoon depicting a hospital ward of recuperating Spideys. Tony Award–winner Alice Ripley tweeted, "Does someone have to die?" and Broadway gossip columnist Michael Riedel was just warming up in the bullpen.

But long before the accidents began and actors found themselves in perpetual defensive postures, there had been disquieting headlines, the kind that exhilarate the acerbic snarky naysayer but also the kind that can mobilize the black clouds of doom from which a show is hard-pressed to escape. And in the ethos of a troubled show where the passing of a week can feel like eternity, the suffering is incontestable.

The *New York Post* and *Variety* scooped it first. There were "cash flow obstacles," which somehow felt euphemistically like a softer gut-punch than "the show is 20 million dollars short." But it was, which seemed implausible because the "sleep-well-children" lullaby sung by the producers had been brass-band emphatic: "The one thing we don't have to worry about is money … the one thing we don't have to worry about is money … the one thing …"

The workshop of the show two years earlier in a New York rehearsal room played like a sweetheart of a piece and everyone wanted a slice of the investment. Why wouldn't they? The pedigree alone was an embarrassment of riches: Julie Taymor, the visionary; Bono and The Edge, the Grammy-winning international superstars; Glen Berger, Emmy Award–winning, clever, and crafty writer. Heavy hitters all and sharp as thumbtacks. Stars and Angel investors fell in line for a piece of it. There were a few notes about things to fix, of course, like the top of the second act needed attention and Marvel Comics, the owner of the brand, had a few quibbles. But, by and large, there was the sense that the show was ace-in-the-hole solid.

Some 12 years prior in *The Lion King* Taymor had wondrously transformed a Broadway stage into African grasslands populated by human representations of indigenous animals. The effect was spellbinding, evocative, and groundbreaking. No one doubted and certainly no one questioned Taymor's wherewithal. But there was a catch, and there could be no misinterpretation or misrepresentation: You, they, all of us playing the game of bringing *Spider-Man: Turn Off the Dark* to the stage, every collective soul, must buy into the vision religiously and without hesitation. And then there was the maxim that hung over production rooms and offices like a commandment: "nobody wants to see a 10-million-dollar *Spider-Man*."

David Garfinkle had been flying solo as money-raiser-in-chief for some time. Tony Adams and Garfinkle together had been co-pilots in the beginning, but the damnedest thing happened way back in 2005: Adams fell unconscious at the precise moment that The Edge was to put pen to paper and sign the contract. Adams was dead two days later of a brain hemorrhage. Garfinkle and Adams had become acquainted in 2001. Adams had had scant experience as a Broadway producer, and some bad breaks at that, but had successfully shepherded Blake Edwards's *Victor/Victoria* to Broadway. Garfinkle was an entertainment lawyer and, through a series of someone-knows-someone-from-way-way-back circumstances, Adams and Garfinkle were granted producing rights by Marvel Comics to produce *Spider-Man* the musical.

And then, like a chain of inevitable, preordained events by the gods of creative greatness, a team emerged. Adams knew Paul McGuinness from the 1970s. McGuinness had been the road manager for an Irish rock band called U2. U2 band members Bono and The Edge lived down the road from Irish scriptwriter Neil Jordan. Neil Jordan's films had been scored by composer Elliot Goldenthal, and Goldenthal was the domestic partner of Broadway and film director Julie Taymor.

And had this cozy collective been tethered together by common vision and comprehension of the limitations of the theatre genre then attached perhaps they might have stayed. But Jordan was a writer for film, not theatre, a fact painfully evident as Taymor relieved him of his duties, which caused no small amount of discord. Glen Berger, primarily a script writer for television and straight plays, impressed Taymor with his imaginative "audition" scene written in one night and with nothing to lose. Berger got the gig and team *Spider-Man* the musical was born, never to be torn asunder. Until a few years, lawsuits, fractured friendships, and multimillions of dollars later.

Once the workshop wrapped, it was time to grapple with the physical production which was going to be unlike any theatre of yesteryear replacing nuts and bolts with algorithms and 3D optics. It was all great in theory but also new and much untried. It was also going to cost a king's ransom, but there again nobody wanted to see a 10-million-dollar *Spider-Man*. Or a bunch of ho-hum stage effects that had been done before. This had to be vanguard or not at all.

A flying workshop plotting flying combat and radical flying effects commenced on a Hollywood soundstage. In the 1950s, Peter Foy had devised a weight/counterweight system to "fly" Peter Pan around the Broadway stage. The contraption was relatively simple, and flying in the theatre remained relatively the same for over 50 years: A harness was placed on the "flying" actor with a thin but mighty cable attached to the back of the harness. Offstage and unseen by the audience, stagehands grunted and growled and sometimes jumped off ladders for necessary leverage, but through what was essentially a sophisticated pulley system theatre flying happened.

The theatre flight for *Spider-Man: Turn Off the Dark* would resemble its predecessor not at all; in the theatre of Julie Taymor, the aerial design would more likely resemble flying on film but for the theatre. There was a problem though; whereas film in a theatrical context manipulates a sequence shot in segments to coalesce, in the theatre it must be a full integration from start to finish. And that had never been done before. Plus it had to be cool as hell.

Scott Rogers had designed the flying sequences for the films *Spider-Man* and *Spider-Man 2*. For Broadway, he adopted technology from professional football game television: A camera suspended by multiple cables that allowed the camera operators to move the camera around the field via remote control. Attached to those cables would not be a camera but a human flying at speeds of over 40 miles per hour. Moreover, whereas Flying by Foy was operated by the pure brute of manpower pulling ropes, flying by Rogers involved complex computer programming that sent directions to equally complex—and incredibly expensive—hardware. If it worked, it would represent a significant leap forward in theatre stagecraft innovation. But would the technology work for the theatre? Nobody knew.

More daunting, what kind of theatre could house what was evolving as a behemoth in every department? Was this a "venue" show more suited for Madison Square Garden? A traditional Broadway house show? Was this piece more akin to Cirque du Soleil than a musical? When pressed to assign the proper "name" for something that had never been done before, the team eventually settled into monikering the show a "circus rock and roll drama."

When production reps, designers, and producers began sniffing around what was then called the Hilton Theatre, that leviathan of all Broadway theatres, the jig was up. *Young Frankenstein* had taken up residence there just over a year earlier, but unlike that other Mel Brooks musical called *The Producers* it had trouble finding a consistent audience and was faltering. When *Young Frankenstein* closed on January 4, 2009, *Spider-Man: Turn Off the Dark* had a home, letting down Julie Taymor who never wanted the show in a traditional Broadway house, so it was reported.

Regardless, a Broadway musical it was even if it didn't play by the so-called rules and was reinventing them as it went along. And with reinvention comes necessary trial and error. Which costs money. But what the heck? "If there's one thing we don't have to worry about it's money."

Until they were 20 million dollars short.

> Rumors have spread among legiters that the production team for incoming mega-musical *Spider-Man: Turn Off the Dark* may be threatened. The extensive work being done to prep for the technically demanding show, both in the shop constructing the physical production and in the theatre where *Spider-Man* is due to bow, is said to have stopped.
>
> Variety, *August 6, 2009*

It went on: "The halt is attributed to cash flow obstacles."

The burn of the U.S. financial crisis in the fall of 2008 had melted the financial markets and taken fortunes with them. Millions pledged by backers that Garfinkle had finagled to capitalize *Spider-Man: Turn Off the Dark* had evaporated, and the moneymen and moneywomen themselves were routinely letting his incoming calls go straight to voice mail. But by now millions were out in contracts and bills were raining in. Production costs and the leasing and readying of the Hilton Theatre weren't all of it; millions more must be held in a bank account to restore the theatre back to its original form whether the show ran 20 years, a day, or not at all.

With best efforts, all efforts really, failing, a demoralized Garfinkle had no choice but to halt production immediately and indefinitely. With renovations stopped, sets unpainted, and costumes unstitched, the actors too were officially released from their contracts. Except for one: Alan Cumming, who had signed to play the Green Goblin, was placed on retainer for when the money showed up, which the production team was certain it would. Until it didn't.

Deep-pocketed rock tour promoter Michael Cohl had a lengthy list of millionaires programmed into his speed dial. Bono and The Edge, being Bono and The Edge, made a few calls. Cohl was tapped to ferry this thing, whatever it was, back out to sea.

By March the show, in spite of having suffered setbacks and pushbacks on dates because of set building issues, technology snafus, casting complications, and, finally, "cash flow obstacles," wobbled back onto the track. The budget had now reportedly ballooned to over 50 million dollars.

The hell of it all was the fact that the show was still a 30-million-dollar musical. *Washington Post* theatre critic Peter Marks was compelled to wonder "where all those tens of millions went" because an astronomical swath of it didn't end up on stage. Rather, it was, according to reports, shelled out in astronomical rent payments to retain the Hilton Theatre, legal fees, retainers, a casting process that was now down the drain, and anything and everything else imaginable.

Shortly before the resumption of work, Cohl cleared the coal-sized lump from his throat and revealed that this elephantine show would require at least 40 stagehands (and counting) to run the backstage tasks and that cost would jack the weekly operating costs to a staggering 1.1 million dollars per week (and counting).

Rehearsals with the full cast (mercifully, many of the originals returned) began in August of 2010. They were to continue for four weeks before technical rehearsals began. Barring no unforeseen circumstances, the show would play its first preview to a live audience on November 6, 2010.

There were unforeseen circumstances.

In a typical rehearsal period for a show, the great majority of what occurs involving the actors on stage is worked out in the rehearsal room, leaving the technical elements to be sorted once the cast arrives at the theatre. Nothing being typical in this *Spider-Man* though, 13 of the then 37 scenes contained in the show could not be rehearsed until the cast arrived onto the set and into the complicated flying harnesses and navigated a labyrinthine of complex costumes, miles of scenery, and a phalanx of stagehands. The show was sitting on a live wire and Taymor knew it but dismissed it as "the nature of the beast." The technical rehearsal period would, out of necessity, have to double as a de facto rehearsal period for more than one-third of the show.

By three weeks into the cast rehearsals, nearly all of the technical hardware had been loaded into the Hilton Theatre and was being methodically readied for population by the actors. This included the ring truss.

The ring truss. The sound of the name of the thing alone induced a twitch in Michael Cohl's lower posterior. It was a colossal contraption that, at the climax of the show, would deploy a massive funnel-shaped spider web over the heads of the audience in which Spider-Man and Arachne would battle to the death. If it worked, it would be a coup de theatre like no one had ever witnessed. If it didn't, it would be a massively expensive screwup like no one had ever witnessed. So, would it work? No one knew. During production meetings, it was posited that a model be built for test purposes. The model would cost around 80,000 dollars and still might not provide conclusive proof one way or another. That plan was scrapped. The other option was to build a scale model of half of it, which also might not prove conclusive. Also scrapped. Finally, the decision was to go all in. In total, the piece would cost one million dollars. It would also be at the center of what would be a great undoing. But that was still months out.

Within a week the ring truss came down, it being apparent that the whole undertaking was a massive misfire. A million-dollar misfire. But the million bucks weren't all that had hurriedly gone up in flames; with the ring truss having been consigned to the trash heap, now there was no finale either.

The first accident happened during technical rehearsals on September 26. It was only a broken toe, but in the theatre "only" can be no casual dismissal; an injury even as uncomplicated as a broken toe is in that context wildly complex and several layers deep. If the actor cannot walk then he or she is likely out of the show for a period of time. This affects not only the livelihood of the actor but the well-being of the show itself, often requiring replacement actors being found and precious rehearsal hours and resources tapped.

In *Spider-Man: Turn Off the Dark,* there wasn't one Spider-Man but several Spideys; Reeve Carney was the actor who played the superhero himself, but behind other identical masks there was a cluster of them, all integral to the purpose of the spider-warrior either being in multiple locales in short order or performing the stunt work of the show. On the occasion of the first accident it was, like so many others, a technical glitch. (Human error would come later and nearly shutter the entire endeavor.)

Brandon Rubendall, one of the flying Spider-Men, was making his Broadway debut. The stunt was complex but cut and dry: At the appointed moment after a set piece had been secured in place, the actor would fly and land on it, completing the move. But in rehearsal, because of a technical glitch, the ramp failed to lower to the proper height and the flying actor slammed into it breaking his toe and causing a hairline fracture to his foot.

Man down.

Later that week during a dance rehearsal another dancer flipped, but his feet didn't make it over to the other side. He landed on his head and was out cold. He was carried from the theatre to an ambulance with his neck in a brace.

Technical rehearsals, the time frame during which all of the technical elements of the show are set and rehearsed, continued at a glacial pace. The mosaic of elements that comprise a Broadway show has grown increasingly more complicated as technology has evolved and *Spider-Man: Turn Off the Dark*, the nonmusical-musical-circus-rock-and-roll-spectacular, was slowly blazing trails and quickly shelling out money. The time required to troubleshoot and implement the technology meant that, as reported by Glen Berger, one hour of technical rehearsals would lock down only approximately 21 seconds of the show. And time is money in show business. The budget continued to bloat. Michael Cohl was taking deep yoga breaths, but he couldn't dwell for long on how much the show was costing. He had bigger problems in the form of unfinished scenes, technology that appeared to have a mind of its own, and an epic, mind-blowing aerial battle between Spider-Man and his formidable rival Green Goblin at the culmination of Act I. The problem there? How could anything in Act II possibly eclipse *that*, especially now that the ring truss had been jettisoned? But Julie Taymor had topped herself before. There was no reason not to extend the benefit of that doubt.

And then, in mid-October, more trouble. The *New York Times* reported:

> A spokesman for the show on Friday confirmed the accident in which Kevin Aubin, a dancer and one of several performers who doubles as Spider-Man in the show, broke both his wrists when he was catapulted into the air—in a kind of sling-shot effect—from the back of the stage to its lip, where he landed with notable force.
>
> *Patrick Healy,* New York Times, *October 29, 2010*

Berger reported it differently. In the version Berger tells, Aubin performed what had been dubbed "The Big Jump." The actor/stuntman leaped forward from a 20-foot-high ramp and after an in-air somersault landed in a crouched position at the front edge of the stage just inches from the audience in the front row. The actor/stuntman would then, at the appointed moment after a set piece had been secured in place, fly and land on it, completing the move. Berger's version turned out to be accurate, making the incident the exact same accident that had injured Rubendall. The redundancy to prevent a repeat of the first accident had failed.

The theatre can be an extremely perilous place; dancers are routinely injured because of the demands placed on their bodies which often far exceed even the most strenuous physical demands elsewhere. Actors have fallen into orchestra pits, down trapdoor openings, and suffered broken feet and limbs and nearly every other conceivable injury large and small. But the *Spider-Man* injuries were game-changers because they occurred within certain heretofore unknown theatre technology that some deemed too untried, too risky, and potentially too faulty.

Michael Riedel, the Broadway columnist for the *New York Post*, swooped in on the story with lightning speed calling it a "bone breaking Spectacle of Insanity." Soon news of the injuries and budget problems of the show was now leaking every-where, toxifying public opinion. Regardless, technical rehearsals pressed forward. There was much more to do, and the first preview was just over the horizon. But the dark cloud over the show persisted like a galling migraine.

As the hours crawled by in technical rehearsals, it became ever clearer that although the clock ticking was getting louder and louder and temperaments in the Foxwoods growing icier and icier, the show itself had tremendous nontechnical problems to be solved too, many of which had been neglected thus far due to the technical issues.

Now, with the tension in the Foxwoods growing ever greater by the day, the decision was made to push the first preview back by two weeks. In doing so, the opening date was pushed too, from December 21 to January 11, missing the cash-cow pre-Thanksgiving tourist onslaught and the Christmas to New Year's crowd that wanted positive reviews before forking over several hundred bucks to see a musical. It was the only option, even if it wasn't a good one.

The press pounced. Riedel's words became more malicious. Healy of the *New York Times* scooped the still nonexistent ending of the show. Word got out that there was a pending visit by the New York State Department of Labor to approve the aerial feats. Since the last thing the show needed was more bad press, Michael Cohl wisely minimized the truth of the matter in an interview with the *Times*: "It's all about tweaking nuts and bolts now, and we're slightly behind, but really it's finally coming together at long last" (Patrick Healy, *New York Times*, November 5, 2010).

In reality, scenes were being rewritten from the ground up, hydraulics were malfunctioning and crushing excessively pricey scenery, and Bono and The Edge were AWOL; they were headed to Australia. But as for the latter, Taymor was non-plussed; she was starting to find that their, as Berger put it, "critiques of an unfinished show" were "becoming a distraction."

A solution to the matter of the missing Act II finale emerged. With the web ring in a landfill now and a Plan B that had also been discarded behind them, it was decided that a gigantic web of netting would be hoisted from the pit upon which the final battle scene between Spider-Man and Arachne would play.

The inclusion of the legend of Arachne as a player in the show had been, was, and would be the Achilles' heel of this *Spider-Man* saga—onstage and offstage. Taymor had insisted on the inclusion and it was a nonnegotiable point; in fact, it was the hook that got Taymor onboard. But the move presented far-reaching challenges. Taymor nevertheless stuck to her guns in spite of the fact that at every conceivable turn all signs were pointing to the inclusion as generating more problems than not.

In Greek mythology, Arachne was a mortal weaver who challenged Athena, goddess of things crafty, Arachne asserting that her skills were superior. For her hubris she was turned into a giant spider. In *Spider-Man: Turn Off the Dark*, Peter Parker, Spidey's alter-ego, is taunted unrelentingly by Arachne, who is eventually convinced that she and Spider-Man were destined to weave themselves into eternity together.

Or some such.

The first paying audience to see *Spider-Man: Turn Off the Dark* arrived, finally, on a crisp late November night in 2010. "I'm hellishly excited" bellowed a fidgety Michael Cohl in the preshow curtain speech to the first-nighters. To hear one cast member describe it, the show that night "was like skateboarding down a mountain of potholes never knowing if the next would jolt the fatal blow, losing the audience entirely." Despite the incessant, too familiar "hold, please" emanating from the stage manager's microphone, the show did reach the bottom and had managed to tell a relatively lucid, if unglued, story.

60 Minutes, the CBS Sunday night news program, had aired a story around the time the intrepid crowd was getting comfortable in their theatre seats tantamount to the best publicity a show could get. Discussing the show in the unabated interview, Michael Cohl had revised upward the magic number of the show's maxim, casually touting that "nobody wants to see a *twenty-five million dollar Spider-Man.*" The sense of intrigue that the *60 Minutes* story had generated for the show had an immediate effect: The story had grossed over 700,000 dollars in advance ticket sales that evening alone. With that news and the first preview behind them, the mood was merrier than it had been in a long while. The show hadn't run perfectly that night but at least, thank God, there had been no accidents or injuries.

Two days later, the cast returned to the theatre after a day off for rest. Backstage, Natalie Mendoza, the actress who played Arachne, made an overdue announcement: She had been struck on the head by a heavy object during the first preview and in the aftermath was still feeling unsteady on her feet. The next day Mendoza reported that her doctor advised time to recover from the concussion. Mendoza would be out of the show indefinitely.

As if the bad press hadn't already damaged the show's reputation, the blogosphere, far less tactful, was now ablaze with reports of the show as the previews began. Everyone seemed to have an angle about how to fix what was murky in the show's plotline, much of it involving Arachne's Act II narrative or her inclusion at all. Taymor refused to read the blogs. With the show now hard-opening on January 11, postponed from December 21, and with critics attending in the week prior, she remained steadfast, holding on to her vision.

Others were privately beginning to whisper among themselves possible solutions to the big and small messes that seemed to lie everywhere. Among the former: The show still had no razzle-dazzle ending and much of the second act, rife with strange dreamlike sequences, even tap-dancing spiders, was all but losing the audience nightly. Not knowing how else to proceed, Cohl made the agonizing decision that the show would postpone the opening once again. February 7 was now the opening night. Cold comfort.

It was December 20 and the entire *Spider-Man: Turn Off the Dark* assemblage of theatre folks was ready for a short breather. It hadn't felt much like the Christmas season to some. With rehearsals during the daylight hours and shows at night, Christmas was nearly an afterthought. A few blessed hours of distraction were going to be most welcome.

Nothing particularly remarkable had occurred during that evening's performance.

The show was beginning to wind down much like that announcement from the pilot that "We are beginning our final approach." The audience, rampant with tourists, had just cheered Reeve Carney's "Boy Falls From The Sky" number and the stage floor was rising as planned to be secured into place. Chris Tierney, one of the Spider-Man stunt doubles, was to mime a slow-motion run on the platform and then jump from it as though jumping from the Brooklyn Bridge to save paramour Mary Jane. His fall would be broken by a safety cable that extended from the back of the stage and was securely fastened to Tierney. That tether was the only element stopping Tierney from crashing into the floor at 40 miles per hour.

The routine was uncomplicated: At the appointed time in the performance, a stagehand would arrive at a designated point backstage where he would find waiting the safety cable and attach one end of it to a secure hook. Next, Tierney would arrive and out of view of the audience the stagehand would fasten the cable to Tierney's safety harness.

It was the simplest of tasks, but damned if that stagehand couldn't find the flashlight that enabled him to see to fasten the safety cable both into the floor and onto Tierney that night. Tierney arrived at the rendezvous point and the stagehand, pressed for time, hastily attached the cable to the stuntman but had neglected to fasten the cable into the hook on the floor. What happened next was calamitous.

The impact fractured Tierney's skull and several vertebrae. A man in lesser tip-top a physical condition would have surely been dead. Tierney was now the most recent unfortunate casualty in a show that was being openly, crushingly touted in theatre circles and the media as "seemingly jinxed."

First responders were at the stage door in minutes and within the hour the press began to buzz around the theatre like a swarm of bees shaken from the hive. The audience had been dismissed moments after the accident but hundreds hung around outside the theatre as curious onlookers. As Tierney was rushed from the stage door to the ambulance, the crowd cheered encouragement. Not knowing if their colleague would live or die, the cast held onto each other, cried in one another's arms, and prayed.

By the next morning, the breaking story was national news. Every New York newspaper ran a story, many as front-page news. Some of it was blistering. Passersby of the ubiquitous New York sidewalk newsstands couldn't help but gander at the front-page tabloid *journalism sensationnel*, the kind that is generally reserved for outing politicians who cavort with prostitutes or exposing rapacious wives of Upper East Side society. But this time it was, of all things, a Broadway show that had been besieged by scandal.

Remarkably, Tierney presented himself to be of the mind that "Hey! Accidents happen," and broadcast from his hospital bed that he was eager to return to the show. His disposition pleased Taymor, who by now must have felt that the theatre community was ready to burst through the barricade and have her drawn and quartered. Since this time human error was to blame, there was only one thing to do: Place a redundancy into the protocol of the live interaction and get back to work.

Bono was in Ireland. Why, after a month in Australia, had he not made tracks back to New York and at once resumed his duties to his fledgling show at the Foxwoods, some wondered. But perhaps not Taymor. Perhaps at this point Bono was merely a surrogate who was fading away; she needed his seed for the songs but she, after all, was gestating the baby. The plausibility of it seemed to be supported by the reports that Taymor was taking advice from no one as to how to save the show from its own woes.

The Edge was as perplexed as the audience when he returned to the show; the ending just didn't make sense. Bono, who upon his return to New York had been ecstatic with the success of the first act, returned backstage after the final curtain, according to Berger, "looking like his dog had just died." Nobody imagined that the present ending, even with revised staging, would sustain a satisfactory ending. Except Taymor.

In fact, Taymor was growing more defensive and brittle by the day, according to reports, ever forestalling other opinions. Later Berger recalled "seeing the iceberg" and practically screaming that it lay ahead and petitioning to divert the boat, but Taymor wouldn't listen to the warnings.

The iceberg was Arachne. The focus of the second act of the show had inexplicably shifted to her story, the strand of the narrative that Taymor had insisted on incorporating, leaving Spider-Man and the entourage in the backseat nearly as secondary characters. Or so it appeared when Arachne sang three songs in a row. Taymor defended the choice. But, in fact, the Arachne trio of songs hardly scratched the surface; Act II was rife with problems. Besides the ever-looming problem of how to resolve the climactic battle finale between Arachne and Spider-Man replete with the infamous web-net that deployed properly sometimes and sometimes not there were eerie dream-invading sequences and disorienting illusions that were confusing to everyone in the place. Except Taymor.

Then there was that other confounding problem involving a musical number called "Deeply Furious" that became known in certain circles as the "shoe song" because of the number of shoes affixed on Arachne's lackey's multiple legs during one scene and song. Imagine the implications. The sheer thought of the song made most cringe outright. Except Taymor. With certain unanimity, the production team wanted the song cut from the show, but Taymor refused—she wanted to expand it.

The co-writers shook their heads. Their careers were on the line, but Taymor appeared to be playing an ego-driven dangerous game by refusing to implement their idea fixes, militantly firing back that they didn't know what they were talking about, and insinuating repeatedly that they were way out of their league. Or so the reports went. She also locked horns more than once with Michael Cohl, once describing him to Berger as a "thug." True, it hadn't been an easy couple of months. Apart from the tumult at *Spider-Man: Turn Off the Dark*, Taymor's film version of *Hamlet* had opened and been panned nearly universally, eventually losing nearly 20 million dollars. If Taymor was shaken, she didn't let on and stuck with her poker face. But privately some wondered if what appeared to be pigheadedness was in reality a wire of self-doubt that had been tripped.

Then, like a band of rebels ostensibly plotting a theatrical *coup d'état*, the writers began to meet privately, without Taymor. The way forward seemed clear and the group's eyes were wide open; Berger had devised a series of snips and a few considerably larger swipes about which everyone agreed would clarify the narrative that was still perplexing audiences eight times a week. If Taymor found out, she would consider the meetings nothing short of blasphemous, as she considered her way forward to be sacrosanct and everyone simply needed to stay calm and trust her vision.

Trust her vision. The words hung in everyone's head like an 11th commandment, but the writers went with their gut. Cohl waffled. The cast was stopping the writers in the hallway, chiming in their two cents about how the show could be saved. Stagehands had their own ideas. The blogosphere was exhausting to follow. Finally, with time and tempers running short, to say nothing of an exhausted cast and crew, Cohl instructed that everyone once again take a deep breath. Opening night was now March 15. A new opening date announcement was placed on the company call-board upon which someone scrawled "yeah, right."

Ben Brantley of the *New York Times* thought it absurd; with the number of previews now in the 60s, the *New York Times* theatre critic saw no reason on earth that preview theatregoers should continue to pay this kind of money to see a show that hadn't been reviewed by the city's most distinguished newspaper. Other critics agreed and purchased tickets for February 5. The online reviews would be published the evening of the 7th and the print reviews on the morning of the 8th. At the Foxwoods, the 7th had been designated as "fauxpening" night.

The reviews were disastrous. Most every critic assailed the plotline as incoherent. The songs were panned for not contributing much to the fleshing out of the characters and for not moving the storyline along. Perhaps the *New York Times* review summed it up for all:

> *Spider-Man* is not only the most expensive musical ever to hit Broadway; it may also rank among the worst… from what I saw on Saturday night, *Spider-Man* is so grievously broken in every respect that it is beyond repair.
> *Ben Brantley,* New York Times, *February 7, 2011*

A stagehand working on the show who was a self-professed dabbler in things dramaturgical had come up with a solution to the show's woes. His ideas made sense and were passed on to Berger, whose mind the reconfigured narrative had already crossed. It involved moving the Green Goblin/Spider-Man air duel to the end of the show, thereby retaining the Goblin as the primary antagonist character throughout the second act. The Arachne illusions would be modified or eliminated and the fallible web-net would be gone for good. The more the team thought on it, the more it felt like the route to take out of this mess, but everyone knew if it were going to happen it had to happen without Taymor, who would refuse. Anarchy was not imminent and Taymor was still a trusted player, but that trust was hanging by a frayed thread. Everyone agreed that the plan would work if it could be executed.

Philip William McKinley also agreed. Cohl brought him around to meet the team. Was it conceivable that McKinley might be brought on board to drive the show to the goal post, which appeared to be moving further downfield by the day? The title of his possible position was yet to be decided, but for now "creative consultant" was being tossed about. The idea was weighty and peppered with guilt. It must have felt nefarious. Cohl suggested to Taymor that she take a three-week vacation during which time changes could be implemented, which she declined to do.

McKinley had only one Broadway credit as a director but several incarnations of the *Ringling Bros. and Barnum & Bailey Circus* show, the latter with short rehearsal periods, which was what *Spider-Man: Turn Off the Dark* needed to get the fixes in. It turned out that options and time weren't all that were running out. The box office take was beginning to wane, and at a meeting on February 26, replete with a lawyer as arbitrator, the team sat at a conference table to decide the next steps. Cohl explained that what had to happen was a matter of "survival," citing the box office decline. Each member of the team offered their thoughts. With no consensus, it was agreed to table a vote until the following weekend when Bono, who attended the meeting via speakerphone, could see the show and the most recent changes. The million-dollar question in the room was whether the show would open as most recently scheduled for March 15.

A meeting without Taymor commenced several days later. The producers, Bono, and The Edge listened intently as Berger walked them through what had been dubbed "Plan X," as though it had leapt from the pages of a cold-war spy novel. They affirmed the plan. Taymor, according to Berger, later railed at the plan, calling it an "incoherent … cut-and-paste mess." Clearly, there was still an insurmountably hideous impasse. Cohl, with little choice, fired Broadway's golden child Taymor.

The *New York Times* headline matter-of-factly called the Taymor firing a "Precipitous Fall." The same article praised her "artistic genius" and celebrated her as a theatre-world "star auteur." At a cast and crew meeting before the curtain went up and the night before the story ran, Cohl briefed the company, diplomatically stating that Taymor was taking a "leave of absence," but within hours it was clear that the parting had been an ugly ordeal. Cohl also revealed what by now had become bitter cliché: The opening night was being moved to June 14.

The actors and crew met with union reps to ascertain if this new delay was even passable according to union rules. It was widely stated in no uncertain terms that among the team, now with Philip McKinley at the helm, there would be no covert ops. Everyone would report directly to McKinley and each department would have a designate who would take that department's needs and viewpoints to the new director.

A co-writer was hired to assist Berger with the task of implementing the new words of "Plan X." McKinley, quite vocal about his disappointment in the score, was asking for rewrites, additions, and remixes. The "Geek Chorus," problem children of the script since forever but Taymor's brainchildren, was eliminated, opening up channels of dialog heretofore not possible. McKinley's visions sought to imbue a friendlier, more family-oriented tone, and many of Taymor's dark hues and pathos were replaced with a sunnier, more family-friendly tapestry. Marvel Comics would surely be pleased and the box office would surely hum along, too.

The revision machine went into turbo overdrive and in overdrive it would remain until the revisions were in place although, according to some, the show was starting to look like a Disney theme park show. Berger blanched. Taymor sent horrified emails. Cohl worried but held his ground. Bono composed and revised upon request, eventually drawing the line on many of McKinley's proposed revisions until Berger explained this new world order, at which time Bono bit his lip.

The unprecedented was really happening. A Broadway show was closing down for a do-over. An out-of-the-theatre workshop was held at a location across town with hired-hand actors and dancers to try out new ideas. Finally, the time came for the cast to sit at a table, just as they had months prior, to read the new script. They held their breath. And then the unimaginable happened; the black clouds that had relentlessly hung in place suddenly, miraculously, began to waft away. One cast member proclaimed that the new version "felt" like a hit. Another noted how much clearer and funnier the story was. Berger appreciated the praise, although privately he felt slightly sickened having been saddled with forced jokes that referenced sitcom stars and Applebee's.

But the panacea would soon evaporate. The tech crew pushed back, collectively stating that they never agreed to nor imagined changes this extensive. The dancers who initially were quietly appreciative that original choreographer Daniel Ezralow had been given the boot (McKinley pushed him out quietly) because of the exhaustion levels and for fear that the dances would be entirely reworked became mortified when new choreographer Chase Brock placed his own "touches" onto the choreography that ranged from unnecessary to ludicrous in some of their minds.

McKinley was suspect too for taking things too far; one production member described it as a scenario where the new director was breaking things that were fixed and fixing things that weren't broken. It was by some accounts a trip to the Mad Hatter's tea party, but the work was getting done and it felt as though light was beginning to peek through from the end of a very long, impossible-to-navigate tunnel. The honeymoon, if there was one, was assuredly over.

Taymor attended opening night despite Cohl's objections. He had been presented with a subpoena by Taymor's legal team just days earlier. The legal battle involved Taymor's past-due royalties, among other squabbles. Cohl was livid, even going so far as to pull the tickets he believed Taymor would attempt to use to slip into the show. She found a way in anyway.

And so it was; after 182 previews, the most of any Broadway show ever, there would be no more delayed openings. *Spider-Man 2.0* (as some had come to call it) opened June 14, 2011. The theatre was filled with A-list stars. When everyone was still milling around and socializing in the lobby at 6:45, Hollywood mogul Harvey Weinstein gruffed, "what time is this show supposed to start anyway?" "6:30," said an assistant. Finally, at 7:15, former US President Bill Clinton was seen being ushered to his seat, flanked by Secret Service agents.

At the curtain call Cohl politely thanked Taymor, who came to the stage. She embraced him. The show was warmly received that night and the critics were mixed but kinder, Brantley stating, "If I knew a less than precocious child of 10 or so, and had several hundred dollars to throw away, I would consider taking him or her to the new and improved *Spider-Man*."

Playbill might have summed the sentiment of the evening up most graciously:

> You gotta hand it to the web-slinger. Circling and soaring and spinning around the cavernous Foxwoods, he really knows how to work a room. And to the star-centric, eclectic group of first-nighters, he was received as the Action Hero they'd been waiting for. It was as though its creators had finally heeded their own subtitle and turned off the dark to deliver a comic-strip stalwart in all his primary colors and glory. And the NYC-saving course of

action he pursued was properly broad-stroked and easy to follow, contrary to the confusing and contorted storyline the critics last reported.

Harry Haun, Playbill, *June 15, 2011*

Berger recalls the relief of receiving performance reports from stage management that described the show that evening as "uneventful." It was a long way from the ulcer-inducing days of a few months prior.

The Shakespearean ordeal was over, but the cast was understandably "shell-shocked," in the words of one cast member. When asked about the tone and disposition of the cast after the show finally opened, the same cast member later reported:

> I mean, they were showing up at half hour call and performing the show, but there were always underpinnings of their long-endured stress. At one point we had to re-light something so we were called in and stood around on the stage in full costume while they tweaked lights. I thought some of them were about to crack—it was like being back there in endless Tech again. Similarly, every time (stage manager) Kat Purvis said, "And we're gonna hold" over the speaker system during the show for all to hear, the cast was instantly on edge. As the originals left and new people replaced them it became less that way and more the usual—what you would expect.

Spider-Man: Turn Off the Dark continued to spin its web, but eventually the more than million-dollar-a-week upkeep caught up with it; for several months prior to closing, the ticket sales had consistently fallen 200,000–300,000 below day-to-day operating costs and the gigantic Foxwoods Theatre had on average only three-quarters of the seats filled. Arena tours, a German production, and a Las Vegas production had been announced. Investors shrugged and hoped they would see some return on their investments, someday. But as one cast member noted:

> We had heard rumors about Las Vegas but most of us were planning our lives post-Spidey, whether it be a new show, new city, or a break. I can't think of anyone who was planning on taking the job if it came along. Spidey had been, for the most part, a great job in the city, but we were excited to try new things.

At the final curtain call the cast held up signs: "Always Bet On Red and Blue!" and "Vegas Baby!" but it was a bet for suckers. As of this writing, no other productions have materialized.

Spider-Man: Turn Off the Dark lost 60 million dollars for all its troubles.

2

LESTAT

Opened April 25, 2006
Closed May 28, 2006

Vampires and musicals make strange bedfellows.

Key dramatis personae

Elton John, Composer: Iconic writer and performer of countless hit pop songs and venerated Broadway musical songwriter (*The Lion King, Aida, Billy Elliot*).

Bernie Taupin, Lyricist: Lauded pop songwriter; first-time original Broadway musical writer for *Lestat*.

Linda Woolverton, Script Writer: Known for work on Disney films and their Broadway adaptations and other Broadway outings.

Anne Rice, Author: Bestselling author of *The Vampire Chronicles* from which *Lestat* is derived.

Robert Jess Roth, Director: Acclaimed director of the stage adaptation of *Beauty and the Beast*.

Matt West, Musical Staging, Actor, and Choreographer: Previously collaborated with Roth and Woolverton on *Beauty and the Beast*.

A promising new contender has arrived in a crowded pharmaceutical field. Joining the ranks of Ambien, Lunesta, Sonata, and other prescription lullaby drugs is *Lestat*, the musical sleeping pill that opened last night at the Palace Theatre.

Ben Brantley, New York Times *Review, April 26, 2006*

Lestat

There might have been a sign in the Palace Theatre lobby addressing the opening night audience with a disclaimer as they advanced into the auditorium:

> Confounding absences of theatrical common sense ahead so consider yourself duly warned.

Let me recount the first of the musical's most salient moments: Lestat, a mortal, retreats from his would-be (male) lover's bedroom in 1778 Paris and quickly becomes prey to an odious vampire who then ceremoniously vanishes into the pyre. Now our Lestat is swiftly and unwittingly transformed into a thirsty fellow bloodsucker vampire. The scene I speak of here is a scene or two later than the one where Lestat is inexplicably renounced by his father (Wolf Killer!) and hence commanded by his mother to go to Paris and make the life for himself that she "never could."

This might not be what she had in mind.

And we are only about 20 minutes in.

There is a trunk full of questions about why anyone thought *Lestat* would make compelling fodder as a stage musical and why. Warner Bros. Theatre Ventures certainly did. In its maiden undertaking, it was at the time attempting to exploit the success of Anne Rice's wildly popular book series entitled *The Vampire Chronicles* by turning it into musical theatre fare. But they were as shortsighted as the noses on their faces (or as blind as the little suckers themselves allegedly are) as the venture didn't take into account that musicals involving anything vampire-ish, the supernatural, and monsters in general were, by and large, problematic in the musical theatre. There was well-documented evidence.

Dance of the Vampires had given it a go on Broadway in 2002 (and is discussed later in this volume) but was handed return voyage back to Transylvania less than two months later. Frank Wildhorn's *Dracula* had winged into the Belasco Theatre in August 2004 but was chased out by broom-brandishing critics and snickering audiences only 254 performances later.

Newsday's Linda Winer, in her review of *Lestat*, summed the situation up: "The undead can't catch a break on Broadway these days … the curse continues with *Lestat*."

There were other shows. Some people, inexplicably, seem to pay no attention to history.

Carrie the musical had unwittingly set something of an accidental precedent. Theatre and the supernatural made for strange bedfellows and got the side-eye from critics and audiences prior to opening night even after the *Carrie* debacle. It seemed that there was a general home-grown wariness from theatre aficionados for much not-of-this-world topical matter, with exceptions.

It wasn't that *Carrie* was atrocious, or, for that matter, that any of the abovementioned musicals were flops void of all artistic merit. In *Carrie*, in particular, there were more than a small number of decidedly appealing elements and even a fair amount dabbling into artistic achievement. But the history lesson and cautionary tale that *Carrie* and others left behind is that, never mind the artistic virtues, the subject matter itself may not be a made-in-heaven fit for a musical. This is largely because there seems nary a good way to do this brand of musical theatre without too often unintentionally resorting to cliché and, worse, "camp," a performance style of its own merits that hangs its hat on artificiality and over-the-top-so-bad-it's-good tastelessness, leaving the audience at sea and repeatedly saying to themselves "they can't be serious." But here I point you to an Elton John (the *Lestat* composer) interview prior to the New York debut of the show:

> We have unified the [Anne Rice] books into a linear storyline and our intention is to make a stylish, sexy, intelligent, and richly hypnotic show that is stripped of gothic clichés and that shows the vampire dealing with his damnation on a more realistic and human level.
>
> Playbill, *April 25, 2006*

John knows how to handily write a score for a musical; he did it brilliantly for *The Lion King*, a show of impressive construct and a musical Venus flytrap for tourists. *Aida*, mostly a handy vehicle for a dandy Elton John score, had woes but became a success largely due to John's contributions. But the problems that *Lestat* presented, conceptually, collaboratively, and otherwise, seemed more than John could save from itself.

Then again, and according to some, if John himself had been more available during the rehearsal process, perhaps the outcome might have been different. Said one cast member: "He was hardly there. He's Elton John and he had commitments. We hardly saw him."

A clear-thinking director can persistently navigate vulnerable topical matter away from straying too far into the "camp" camp (Harold Prince did it splendidly with *The Phantom of the Opera*), but without vigilance it too often becomes rehearsal quicksand; before you know it you've slipped in up to your chin, and the feeling of doom in the air of the rehearsal room is infinitely more terrifying than the doom in the air of any "goth" musical you're producing.

But even an able and vigilant director is nonetheless at the mercy of the lyric and book writer(s). If the director and writers aren't hinged to one altogether about how the story is told and aren't able to dodge the inevitable traps, a show can get in a conceptual pickle. *Lestat* had a lyricist, Bernie Taupin, and a separate book (narrative, script) writer, Linda Woolverton, and Taupin, a neophyte lyric writer for the theatre, took a lot of heat from the show's critics, with claims that his work on *Lestat* wasn't up to Broadway standards.

But Taupin can't be overly blamed; he wrote much of *Lestat* in the pop music vernacular he was accustomed to. It seems that no one pressed the fact that theatre lyrics require a narrow specificity, situationally driven and dictated by the individuality, language, syntax, thought processes, intentions, and dispositions of the characters who sing them, which, in most cases, is simultaneously and ideally moving the plotline ahead. By contrast, pop songs may tolerate extensive use of metaphor and heavy use of the abstract, are mostly situation and not character dictated, and, in most cases, are not responsible for linear narrative of a storyline. A theatre lyric not grounded in the sensibility of character-sung *moment-to-moment* and inclusive of extensive metaphor or flowery language demands that the audience unscramble the words too extensively in order to follow along with the narrative.

Moreover, no shortage of lyrics in the show suffered from the "partial-rhyme" syndrome which occurs when the vowels in the words match (rhyme) but the consonants (or combinations of consonants) differ. Many lyric writers pull this off with flair and the ear doesn't mind, but out of some lyric writers' pens can come soggy, forced, and smack of approximated intent.

Whatever distractions the lyrics created could have, to some sizable extent, been abated and offset by script writer veteran Linda Woolverton. Audiences know her exemplary accomplishments through Disney films, notably *Beauty and the Beast* for which she adapted her own screenplay for the stage version and subsequently was honored with a Tony Award nomination. Chances are she also felt it was good luck that *Lestat* was playing in the same theatre on Broadway that her previous shows had played and scored. Turns out that with Broadway musicals, when the show isn't working, luck usually hides. If one really catches a break, then luck will make a welcome reemergence in the aftermath of the slaughter as musical show people hope their names will be absent from the naughty list in the media reporting on the show and the naysayers about town.

In a musical, the book writer's typical job description includes shepherding the storyline into a contoured, intuitive, and relatable narrative. The book writer must clarify, at every turn, any confusion (unless it is intentional as a dramatic device) that the audience might have in terms of the storyline itself and the elements therein. Moreover, the book writer must be responsible for the spoken dialog in the musical and must provide a seamless narrative from which the lyric writer crafts the words to the songs.

The opening minutes of *Lestat* eschewed some of these golden rules right out of the starting gate, racing the narrative, murky to begin with, and hardly giving the audience time to process it. The moment is one of more than a handful that leaves the audience, certainly those not acquainted with the Rice "vampire" series, scratching its collective head.

Regardless, the opening played more effectively than the out-of-town San Francisco tryout version, a time period before a show opens in New York for the show to play before an audience to gauge what "works" or "plays" well for the audience and what does not. There the show's opening was set in modern day with Lestat buttoned up neatly attired in a fashionable three-piece designer suit. Lestat announces that he has a unique story to tell and promptly seats himself at his laptop and begins to type. Uncomfortable laughter trickles from the audience as they don't appear to know for certain if they are witnessing comedy or drama, realism or camp. The opening is later scrapped and replaced with the present version.

Lestat sojourns to Paris at his mother's insistence and once there in no time flat has reunited with pal Nicolas, an actor in a Parisian theatre who keeps company with a free-spirited lot all having come to Paris, so they declare, to "liberate our lives!," a point that is pressed mercilessly by ceaseless talk of ménage a trois (I'll bring a friend!), jealous lovers ("Whore! Trollop!"), and unbridled lust ("I'd give my meager wages for a roll with that young stranger there!"). Straightaway the lyrical gesture has betrayed the vision John appears to have set forth and has degraded an integrity that might have better served John's of a "stylish, sexy, intelligent, and richly hypnotic show."

Lestat and Nicolas arrive at Nicolas's paltry room. There's a little teasing, a little boy-wrestling. Then that voice of the father is again booming in Lestat's noggin. "WOLF KILLER!" it screams.

Lestat excuses himself and steps outside into the Parisian night. Aforementioned salacious vampire named Magnus appears from the flames. Blinding red light and smoke. Ominous music. Enormous climax of sensory elements on all counts. We learn that Magnus has selected Lestat for vampire immortality after witnessing Lestat's valiant encounter fending off the wolves. Magnus strikes and almost immediately Lestat develops a gluttonous thirst.

Gabrielle is now in Paris and the narrative whipsaws past Lestat's dilemma to his reunion with his sickly mother who matter-of-factly states that she "has come to Paris to die." It doesn't take a mother's intuition to realize that Lestat has changed, and he reveals to his mother that "I was taken. The gothic legend (of the vampire) is true." Nearly without pause Gabrielle pleads with Lestat to "make me as you are!" and excitedly claims that the two will, as vampire immortals, live "under the stars" forever and together.

Call it a son's love or an excuse to keep the Gabrielle narrative aloft, Lestat agrees and gives Mother the bite. Awash with rejuvenation Gabrielle scoots and scampers about the stage like a schoolgirl, chopping her hair off, delighted. Later as she writhes in pain (she doesn't seem to mind, really), Lestat tells her that her body is dying. Soon she thirsts and attacks a passerby like a rabid beast bathed in febrile, scarlet lighting.

Until this point in Act I, the show looked very different in the San Francisco iteration and for the better, which, for any out-of-town try-out "test" period that it was, is counterintuitive. Following the early version of the opening scene that was axed (remember the laptop?), the creatives felt it necessary to go back to work on the scenes that immediately followed, apparently unhappy with what netted them as well. One of the "improvements" was the signature "blue" sequences (also discussed below) but the optics for the settled-upon version drew unfortunate, unintended laughter (remember "they can't be serious"?) and Gabrielle's first outing as a hungry immortal landed on stage as (there is no other word) "camp."

Lestat and Gabrielle ponder the existence of God, a constant narrative point repeated with such frequency it feels equivalent to a child in the backseat repeatedly asking "Are we there yet?" every mile or two. The pair finds themselves in a church sanctuary where they meet a 300-year-old vampire named Armond who offers them a sanctuary of a different sort: One "of (their) own kind." Shortly thereafter the scene shifts into a dank vampire den where the night creepers sequester themselves, believing that they are not entitled to roam about freely enjoying the same worldly pleasures as the mortals do. On the contrary, Lestat asserts, and the vampire troupe vows to hide in plain sight by transforming themselves into (what else?) a troupe of actors.

Soon enough the gang is performing a play within a play narrative history of the vampire and for the next eight minutes or so we are saddled, wiggling about in our theatre seats and wondering if we'll ever get out of this mess we're in. The sequence, which can only be called "The Small House of Uncle Vampire," was so reminiscent of the Jerome Robbins ballet in *The King and I* that it's all but impossible not to draw the comparison or at the very least ponder the broader points of copyright infringement.

Then again, maybe we're missing the point. Or maybe we just can't see well enough to discern the difference owing to the fact that, for the better part of 45 minutes, we've been nearly in the dark. Roth at some point must have realized that maybe *Lestat* could have been subtitled "someone please turn on the lights" but there again perhaps he was loathe to reveal how barren the stage seemed to be.

By accounts, much of the scenery and effects once in the show were abandoned by the time the show reached New York, the production team instead favoring reliance on the performances and the narrative itself. Among the ditched technical effects was a generous use of multimedia film, both animated and live action, that was monikered the "Swoon." Writer Evan Henderson described the swoon thus:

> The ecstatic loss of consciousness experienced by both the vampire and his victim, and a key descriptive element of Anne Rice's *The Vampire Chronicles* novels … A man or woman dies, which happens quite a few times in the new musical *Lestat*, and proceeds to enter immortality via a multimedia film. We the audience also take the journey—sometimes just for a second, other times longer—beginning in the blood vessel and gradually making our way through an urgent flashback via a key incident or set of incidents within the person's life.
>
> *Evan Henderson,* Stage Directions Magazine, *March 2006*

The question of whether or not the multimedia and scenic deletions served the show artistically is more arguable than the question of whether or not the inclusion would have served the show commercially. Eye candy is a potent aphrodisiac to an audience, certainly the tourist crowds; at times when a show is flailing, a great looking physical production can often save the day. In other words, even if they leave humming the scenery at least you've given them something to hum. In this final iteration, Lestat became a minimalist product of dim, dingy, and somber.

Nicolas is discovered among the actor-vampires having been abducted by Armond, and Lestat transforms him too. It doesn't work out well. Nicolas is rendered into a catatonic state.

Years pass. Lestat has feverishly looked for Marius, the wise one, to emancipate Nicolas from his still-catatonic state, but the old vampire has remained elusive. Gabrielle again admonishes Lestat to "find a new life for yourself" and seek "meaning." Lestat cannot, as his loyalty to Nicolas persists. But Gabrielle has acquired an untameable vampire wanderlust and asserts that the "wonders that the world can offer" now eclipse "ancient family trees" because "mystery calls" and she "can't resist." When Gabrielle sings "Crimson Kiss" in straightforward language more appropriate for a character and situational plot-driven narrative, the show stirs and livens. This is most welcome, allowing us a bit of letup from an otherwise lumbering Act I. The gesture is not too little but comes too late. Nevertheless, John's appealing melody is confection and Taupin's lyric is awash with pathos and imagination. Lestat implores the restless Gabrielle to stay but she refuses. He finally realizes that a vampire mother has to do what a vampire mother has to do and he releases her with his blessings, instructing her to "take the fire from the moon and run with it!" Good thing for her, but not for us. Gabrielle is a sturdy branch that we, the desperate, reach for while being recklessly hurled down this rocky river.

Nicolas begs Lestat "release me" in a most feeble tone and Lestat finally relents as ominous voices descend from the darkened night sky and into the fire Nicolas goes.

Marius appears in a flash of light and spectacle. Act I is over, but if you came to the theatre tonight looking for entertainment, the real show is just beginning and the reddest hot ticket in town is happening just a few feet from here. Just outside the theatre in the outer lobby, audience members rifle through their *Playbills* and the real merriment begins with the inevitable banter question from one audience member to another: "What do you think of the show?"

And then light as Act II begins. A spirited, splendid production number. Lestat is in New Orleans and the creoles exalt "welcome to the new world!" The locals cut up and celebrate.

Lestat is renewed and unbound. The New Orleans nighttime air is disagreeably thick and generates a paste-like sweat even into the darkest hours when a vampire carries out his sinister deeds. In hardly the time it takes to shuck an oyster, Lestat is liquoring up in the company of the weak and distressed Louis. Lestat and Louis later live together as lovers (and vampires) but Louis begins to protest the arrangement and the (yawn) obligations and mundanities of daily life as one. Lestat tosses it off: "Embrace it!!" Lestat sings. Over and over. And over. While Nicolas attempts with little success to put on his happy face, Lestat is discovering Claudia, a shabby young wretch of a thing skittling about the streets of New Orleans as her mother is dying. Lestat offers "help" and the gesture shocks Claudia: "Are you an angel?" she asks. When Lestat eventually proposes that he and Louis adopt the child, Claudia professes "I have never had a father before and now I have two!" The turn of plot stems some of the critic's most acidic cracks:

The closest *Lestat* comes to so-bad-it's-good camp is in a subplot that might be called "Claudia Has Two Daddies." Claudia is the little orphan girl brought home as a peace offering to the sulking Louis by Lestat, who turns her into a vampire after finding her destitute on the streets of New Orleans.

Ben Brantley, New York Times, *April 26, 2006*

"There's no love like a mother's love, especially if your mom happens to be a vampire. Unless, that is, you have two fathers among the living dead," Gardner wrote. "Those are just a couple of the twists on family values that threaten to make Lestat ... the religious right's worst nightmare" (Claudia Parsons, Reuters).

Two dads with their own bloody agendas surely can't be expected to keep a steady eye on the impish teen, and this turns out to be a downer for the servants and tutors on whom Claudia unleashes her ravenous appetite: "I want more!" she stresses repeatedly in her second-act star-turn.

Thirty years pass as the projection on the downstage curtain tells us, and having grown long weary of those blasé days and nights on the plantation as vampires, Louis and Claudia desire a European excursion to search for "others of our kind." Lestat refuses to allow it and he and Claudia quarrel. "You made me because you are afraid to be alone." She shrieks, "It was for yourself. Always for yourself."

The truthfulness of the Claudia gesture reminds us of the fundamental basis of dramatic structure and the premise that within said set of principles lies a basis of clashing wills, presumably between two or more forces that have a thing or two to gain if the opposing side relents. Naturally, if the forces in opposition push against one another for a reason intuitive to the observer then the dramatic action is more likely to capture and hold the observer's interest. John's statement that the intention of the creatives was to place the characters' struggles on "a more realistic and human level" was well meaning but not entirely realistic on the basis that so little of the content of *Lestat* the musical was empathy-worthy, not because the struggles onstage weren't credible under the character's circumstances, but rather they were not relatable under ours. And there lay the fundamental flaw—if you didn't buy into the premise of Anne Rice novels, *Lestat* the musical was a tough sell. When Claudia confronts Lestat, it is the first moment in the musical that *felt* like a relatable event to most of us mortals and was a transparent reminder that *Lestat* the musical, as played, had a very limited audience share.

Elsewhere in the act as Claudia sings of never having the chance to be a wife, feel a mother's love, or live a conventional life, all due to her transformation, the above points are reinforced but by now the change in tone that the show has taken, a far more relatable one, is too late. Claudia claims that she wishes to "make peace," but it is a ruse and she rages at Lestat, brandishing a knife and threatening his life. Lestat declares that he refuses to "die this way" and escapes the home, confessing his failings and selfishness: "I ungraced the blessed."

In want of telling his prodigal story, Lestat returns to the theatre in Paris to discover that Louis and Claudia have (what else?) joined the acting troupe. Lestat reveals to Armand that while living in the new world a vampire had tried to murder him, and Armand discovers that the would-be murderer was Claudia. Enraged, Armand and company declare this "the greatest of all crimes … to kill your own!" As a result of her treasonous high crime the chanting crowd executes Claudia. Lestat implores Louis to return with him to New Orleans where the two may find solace in one another, but Louis is broken and declares that the world is "one bleak ruin of ashes and death." Lestat commands Louis not to "go into the fire!" But Louis is gone.

Lestat to God: "Every bit of me is broken. My body, my mind, my heart." Lestat asks God to take him. Marius appears and commands Lestat to stand. He is healed. Angel choir. Lestat reappears in modern clothing stating, "I am the vampire Lestat and I will live forever." He turns upstage. Curtain.

Lestat the musical's artistic tree wasn't all barren. Present and accounted for were interesting ideas and theatrical undertakings that made for appetizing provisions from an observer's perspective. And it wasn't guilty of not craftily spinning these out in a comprehensible way. It can't even be said that the musical didn't strive to take a critical stab at musicalizing a popular culture phenomenon. Anne Rice's *The Vampire Chronicles* were best sellers and well known all over the globe. But for all the virtues, scattered and bleak though they may have been, the cardinal absences were fundamental and glaring: There was no real accessible love story, leaving the struggles of the characters to be not romantic but existentialist in nature and in breadth. Moreover, even in the absence of a love story, audiences tend to crave essentially the same familiarities, especially the un-theatre connoisseurs who come in for the pure entertainment of it.

At least one cast member had a simpler take on why the show wasn't a hit. "They [the audiences] of Anne Rice fans came in droves to see us. They were hollering and cheering. There just weren't enough of them." The cast member went on to point out that the show landed just a few years shy of a resurgence of interest in vampire stories due to the popularity of *The Vampire Diaries*. Had the television show been in the mainstream then perhaps *Lestat* would have become more than that "gay vampire musical." Also this was at a time when the TKTS (half-price) ticket booth had temporarily been displaced out of a direct view of the *Lestat* marquee. One cast member suspects that if the tourists waiting in line to buy half-price seats had seen Elton John's name on the marquee perhaps that fact might have generated a great deal more in ticket revenue.

In the pre-Broadway tryout of *Lestat* in San Francisco, the creators might have realized that what was truly relatable to an audience in *Lestat* was being eclipsed by special effects and had taken the gamble to strip the effects away and restore the story and show to a naturalistic narrative with primacy placed upon the character struggles. But the truth was that the effects were more likely interesting, certainly more relatable, than those struggles. They may have even given a proviso for the show to have worked, one that suggested that the show was a fantasy excursion inviting the audience to come along, suspend disbelief, and consume the experience for what it was. The revision was an admirable throw of the dice, but ultimately one that possibly made *Lestat* one of the only musicals in Broadway history that was more palatable out of town.

3

URBAN COWBOY

Opened March 27, 2003
Closed May 18, 2003

Sometimes a show just can't catch a break.

Key dramatis personae

Aaron Latham, Author of original article upon which the film version of *Urban Cowboy* was based, screenwriter of the film, and book writer of *Urban Cowboy* the musical.

Lonnie Price, Actor and Director: Director of the Broadway incarnation of *Urban Cowboy*.

Jason Robert Brown, Composer and Lyricist: Wrote original musical material for *Urban Cowboy* on Broadway and conducted the onstage band.

Jeff Blumenkrantz, Composer and Lyricist: Wrote original musical material for *Urban Cowboy* the musical.

Melinda Roy, Choreographer: Garnered a Tony Award nomination for her work on *Urban Cowboy* the musical.

Phillip Oesterman, Director: Shepherded the show from the beginning through the first workshop.

Chase Mishkin, Lead Producer and indefatigable champion of *Urban Cowboy* the musical.

Urban Cowboy, at the Broadhurst Theatre, is a plodding, ear-splitting attempt to cash in on an American infatuation with honky-tonk and the Texas two-step. If the movie was mostly an excuse for some smoldering lip-lock by its stars, plus a bit of dangerous gyrating on a mechanical bull, the musical is neither as sexy nor as menacing. The time passes as if you were killing an evening in a loud bar with gabby strangers you're increasingly itchy to ditch.

Peter Marks, Washington Post, *April 16, 2003*

Urban Cowboy

Goshdangit. Judd sure comes within spittin' distance of outbiddin' Curly for Laurey's picnic basket at the box social, but Curly wins it after selling his horse and saddle to get the cash. That was *Oklahoma!* in 1943. A few decades later and jus' down the road a piece in Houston, Texas, it's a mechanical bull ride at a lowdown dive called Gilley's that gets 'er done. Those dyed-in-the-wool farm boys sure know how to impress the ladies.

Gilley's is the sort of unpretentious sawdust-carpeted taproom that you mightn't want your momma to know you frequented on a regular basis, but it's where all your pals hang out and kick back a few after a nettlesome day of cow tendin', bottle cap sortin', or assembly line workin'. There's a live band twanging on the bandstand under a neon sign reminding the crowd that "This Bud's For You" while they go plum hog wild line dancing and hollering it up. Turns out that much of the free-wheeling clientele also go there for entertainment of the boots-off variety.

Buford Uan Davis, a young and strapping buck nicknamed "Bud" on account of his initials, rambles into town by way of a small town called Spur, jockeying to make enough money to buy his own farm. Naturally, Bud turns up at Gilley's and beds two women locals that very night. Guess those Texas boys move faster than a heifer out-scooting a lasso, too. The next day Bud reports to work at the oil refinery where his uncle has secured a job for him and becomes acquainted with no-nonsense Sissy. Only love, the hard kind, could possibly happen next.

Urban Cowboy, if you think on it, wasn't a lousy idea for a stage musical that was by all past indications predestined to fail. The show shared DNA with a previous Broadway hit called *Footloose* in that both were hit films prior to becoming stage musicals and both had plots—and mindsets—fixed in rural locales, denizened with rural folks singing appealing contemporary music that underscored their lives and the goings-on in the narrative. *Footloose*, about an urban teenager pressing boundaries of conformity in a two-horse town (this one called Beaumont), may not have been high art but it did have a healthy Broadway run between 1998 and 2000. But then again, when a show provides an audience with a few whoop-ups and a score of hit songs, who needs high art? The success of *Footloose* in New York generated a national tour and a deluge of international, regional, stock, school, and community productions.

Other shows entrenched in rural sensibilities have racked up terrific enthusiasm and some have cleaned up as whopper hits: *The Best Little Whorehouse in Texas* was a guilty pleasure that rounded up an impressive 1,500-plus performances on Broadway and also fared well outside of New York. Those Texas Aggies football boys stirred up a hell of a ruckus, singing about "whompin" and "stompin" it up tonight at the Chicken Ranch, that den of iniquity, where Miss Mona, the hard-boiled madam, keeps her girls shipshape and mindful of their p's and q's.

Songwriter Carol Hall wrote a golden gilded score that gracefully and playfully captured the situational content and managed to chuckle at itself all the while. Moreover, as is the mandate in traditional musical theatre formats, each song guided and supported the narrative.

Annie Get Your Gun, the show Irving Berlin almost didn't write because he "didn't know how to write 'Hillbilly music,'" is a household brand name with an altogether irresistible spirit. Country bumpkin sharpshooter Annie may not have known much about the finer things in life but what she did know got her by just fine.

Notwithstanding Ethel Merman's star turn as the original Annie and subsequent Annies who also sprinkled stardust, the show itself is as solid as five-day-old country cornbread, and the songs all deftly defined character and informed the forward motion of the narrative. Berlin and scriptwriters Dorothy and Herbert Fields were practitioners of the highest order.

At the top of the heap is the aforementioned *Oklahoma!*, which signaled the dawning of the age of the modern musical by being one of the first to reveal songs directly akin to the specifics of the characters who sang them and the particular circumstances they found themselves in.

Given rural musicals' appeal and pedigree, *Urban Cowboy*'s hayseed sensibilities had statistics on its side that on the shiny surface looked sure-footed. It also had a deep-seated potential audience of tourist escapist seekers, many from the South and Midwest. But there was more good news: Country music albums in 2002, the year that *Urban Cowboy* opened, had upward of 50 million albums sold domestically, and country music was the fuel in the engine of the show.

Well, then, what went wrong? The likely answer in part is that there were a lotta bulls at that rodeo potentially bucking the show in opposing directions. By count, there were over 30 songwriters. That many gunslingers aren't as alarming in certain jukebox musicals that may or may not have a fixed storyline, but within the confines of a linear plotline this many voices can at best struggle for clarity and purpose in a narrative. The result was predictable: Many of the songs in the lineup by default became musical scenery, only feebly driving the plotline forward and most settling as background support for another line dance, misunderstood looks between characters, or for a herky-jerky romance to bloom. Even the presence of crackerjack show tunesmiths Jason Robert Brown and Jeff Blumenkrantz, who both did admirable work in an attempt at cohesion, was undermined by country-pop musical numbers elsewhere, all written by artists of that genre, that were flimsily placed and only loosely moved the story along.

The musical theatre of Jason Robert Brown is nothing to shake a stick at. His *The Last Five Years*, *Parade*, and other musical theatre properties are some of the canon's most intriguing; moreover, he has an uncanny talent for writing dense folk and folk-rock songs that transport an otherwise relatively simple medium into an intellectual and visceral event.

Blumenkrantz is also formidable, but a different breed of songwriter. His artistry often lies in wittily tickling at topics of a more "slice of life" variety but not necessarily less relevant.

Consistency is too often the stepchild of craft in theatre writing; as *Urban Cowboy* suggests, even with crafty writers onboard, the work of those who are clearheaded about how to shape a musical can suffer at the hands of inconsistency. A show with 30 songwriters, crafty though they may individually be, is hard-pressed to achieve a set of consistent, even objectives, particularly as pop music is situationally driven above being character driven. With all the swirling about, it may be fair to say that shows in this precarious position often die at the hands of too many doctors around the operating table.

It was reported that the original intent of book writer Aaron Latham and director Phillip Oesterman was to offer Clint Black, the venerable country songwriter, the task of writing the songs. Perhaps uncertain of his own wherewithal at writing musicals, he declined. The eventual solution, as the writers saw it, was a catch-as-catch-can hodgepodge of some original musical material by Nashville songwriters with other country hits plugged in as needed that could somehow be of service to the storyline. Later, Brown and Blumenkrantz were brought on to clarify and navigate the narrative, such as it was, writing original songs in service of the effort.

Unsurprising was the net: A few songs laid a linear path to get the story told, supported the characters' trajectory and struggles, and carried the narrative as a libretto (the sum total of all the words, dialog, and lyrics) should. The others, mostly all stand-alone country songs, were tasked with holding up the narrative.

After a speedy courtship, Bud and Sissy wed. Bud, despite the pleas to pull back the reins by his aunt, is smitten by Sissy and convinced that she'll make the ideal wife. But from rosy trailer park bliss thorns quickly emerge, and back at Gilley's, quick as a Texas tornado, the two soon become convinced that the other is intent on going astray. And lickety-split Bud falls into the arms of Barbie-Doll Pam, a rich West Texas daddy's girl who sings a song about "Dancin' the Slow Ones With You." It's all in an attempt to add some feeling to an otherwise now-languishing plotline.

Sissy enjoys the company of Wes, a brutish escaped convict with a knife and who knows what else. Words and blows are traded and some line dances happen and Uncle Bob develops a nasty cough. You can guess where that last strand of plotline is headed.

Not so much happens next but dribs and drabs. There's some hemmin' and some hawin'. But really that's about it for a while.

What to do in the musical theatre when the plotline runs dry and you've already added a plot element that didn't exist (remember that cough?) was the question. The answer? Dance and then line dance some more.

So they line danced. And some of it was truly thrilling, even winning the praise of the Tony Awards Nominating Committee who graced the show with a Best Choreography nomination that year.

When Oesterman tapped Latham to musicalize the film, the source material was second generation. Latham had delivered an article for *Esquire* magazine some years before chronicling the happenings at a juke joint in Texas (Gilley's). He had become intrigued in part by the changing sexual dynamics of the era and locale and by the idea that riding a mechanical bull was, in part, the face of new Western masculinity and, as it turns out, feminine equality. The film version was directed by James Bridges and the plotline spun out, but some critics felt the film version went amiss.

> The finer possibilities have been betrayed in the film adaptation contrived by Latham and director James Bridges as an absurdly upbeat romantic vehicle for John Travolta. The film-makers appear to believe that the moviegoing public craves a reassuring love story, at any cost.
>
> *Gary Arnold,* Washington Post, *June 11, 1980*

Urban Cowboy the musical had its origins around a dining room table in Latham's New York penthouse. After an early reading Mike Nichols, the celebrated producer and director with a keen eye for a hit, put up cash for further development and eventually was instrumental in getting producers onboard for a workshop. In the theatre, a workshop is akin to a staged rehearsal where creatives have a chance to look at and hear the material "on its feet" and potential investors are invited to attend and determine whether the show is an endeavor that they wish to gain exposure to financially.

At that stage, the show had no original songs, only plug-in country hits that prosaically supported the story. "It was terrible," said one producer, but there were mitigating circumstances: The concept was solid even if the construct was not. Director Oesterman could hardly be blamed: Health issues had become a serious distraction for him and stymied his vision for the show. "He was unfocused," said the producer, going on to suggest that this was understandable given Oesterman's state of health. The workshop didn't set any investment into motion. In fact, the reception in the hallway postperformance was more like the lamentations at a funeral wake than a celebration.

Oesterman had made a number of unique but curious choices. In a typical musical inclusive of an "ensemble," a term that refers to a collective of actors who typically sing and often dance, the group acts as a supportive mechanism to the principal actors and contributes to the moving narrative of the storyline. The *Urban Cowboy* workshop did have an ensemble but those actors remained largely mute; at the appointed times, most often in the Gilley's nightclub sequences, the group would saunter on stage, line dance for a spell, and then largely disappear until the next nightclub sequence. This meant in essence that the ensemble was purely decorative. But to that end so were the songs. Oesterman and Latham had essentially cherry-picked a load of country hits and plugged them into the script, fashioning them to support and comment, placing them throughout the story. The outcome was fatal. "It was a disaster," said one of the show's producers on reflection. "The crème-de-la-crème of the musical theatre world were all there looking at us like we had lost our minds."

But then came an angel. The Coconut Grove Playhouse in Miami, Florida, a 1920s Paramount movie house turned legitimate theatre in the 1950s, had a show drop from its season roster. Coconut Grove producer Arnold Mittelman agreed to present the world premiere of *Urban Cowboy*, and the show was retrieved from the gallows; the demise of the show was not imminent as long as funds were behind it. The commitment to mounting a full production at the Coconut Grove ensured that the show would get a life, presumably inclusive of the herculean revisions needed to make it stage-ready. As time would tell, the move would not be the last or only stay of execution for *Urban Cowboy* the musical.

Sets and costumes were designed. The show was recast from what had been universally agreed upon as a miscast workshop. Revisions of the script and musical material were underway. There was promise and, what's more, a sliver of white light peeking under the doorway that had ostensibly been shut after the workshop failed to incite much interest from investors.

But then Phil Oesterman died in the summer, a few weeks before rehearsals were to begin, at age 64. *Urban Cowboy* was in trouble. Again. With Oesterman no longer attached to the show, the vision of the show might be conceived anew with a new director; but meanwhile, in Florida, the physical production of the show was being built according to the specifications of the Oesterman vision, fuzzy though it might have been.

Lonny Price, until that time best known for his origination of the role of Charley Kringas in the ill-fated Stephen Sondheim show *Merrily We Roll Along* and for his writing, directing, and starring in a charmer of a show called *A Class Act*, which had a short Broadway life but an appreciable following, was offered the director title. He declined based on other commitments citing not enough preparatory time. He did, however, having seen the workshop, agree to meet with Latham to offer dramaturgical advice.

They say that the fireworks that light up an open Texas night sky can be seen clear up to Tulsa. And so it was. Latham and Price got on, as Southerners used to say, like a house afire. Price agreed to direct.

Up until now, *Urban Cowboy* the musical had the makings of a country jukebox musical with an intertwined storyline thread and the two cried for concrete consolidation. Price's highest order was to devise a seamless integration of the two with the tools and materials available. But the pickings were slim, and Price was at the mercy of retrofitting prewritten country hit songs. It couldn't be sensibly done, he thought, certainly not in a way that made for a traditional musical theatre vehicle. Price wouldn't go down the misguided road that his predecessor had. Blumenkrantz, was tapped and turned in several songs that served the integration of storyline and music, notably the introductions and "framing" of the characters. When it became clear that the original musical director of the show wasn't the right fit, Jason Robert Brown was hired. Brown not only musical directed and orchestrated the existing musical numbers, he smartly filled in the holes in the narrative that should be song-driven with his own original song material. The result of the appropriations was positive: The dialog into song was filling out to resemble a traditional narrative.

The outlook was not as sunny in south Florida. The company arrived at the Coconut Grove Playhouse to a hell of a mess. The theatre had overestimated its abilities to get the set built in time let alone how to get the mechanical portions of it operational. "The turntable didn't turn and the bull didn't buck," said one producer. Price added that "every day there was another disaster." In the theatre, when technical elements are gridlocked for one reason or another, the whole show can come to a standstill until the technical problems are solved. This fact is especially problematic out of town; the necessary fixation on the technical components impeded at best and precluded at worst the work that needed to be done to make the show better. The entire production team was livid.

The first act of the first preview performance of *Urban Cowboy* the musical ran the duration of two hours and twenty-five minutes. There were stops. And starts. And more stops. But then in early November as the unmerciful south Florida heat mellowed and waned, *Urban Cowboy* was, by all accounts, a hit. "They (the audience) were cheering and screaming," said Price, "that it was the best thing they've seen in 10 years."

Many of the south Florida critics echoed the audience responses, turning in devastatingly handsome reviews. Jack Zink of the Fort Lauderdale *Sun-Sentinel* was giddy over the show:

> [*Urban Cowboy*] nearly kicks the doors off the Coconut Grove Playhouse in downtown Miami en route to a hoped-for stampede to Broadway later this season ... [The show] seems to want to be *The Best Little Whorehouse in Texas* and *Fool for Love* at the same time, and son of a gun if it doesn't come close.
>
> Sun-Sentinel, *November 18, 2002*

The show ran four weeks in Florida and left town in a blaze of glory. If troubleshooting the technical elements in Miami had rendered little time for the show to be improved upon, so be it; there was "there" there, so everyone thought, and since a Broadway bow now seemed inevitable, time to fix the show's script woes could be built into the schedule before the Broadway opening.

Or so they all thought.

Producers secured the storied Broadhurst Theatre for the Broadway run. A revival of *Into the Woods* had been stationed there but was closing. It was a lucky break for *Urban Cowboy* because the theatre, aside from being a magnificent structure with a rich Broadway history, had a high tourist visibility situated on West 44th Street next to the Shubert and across the way from the St. James Theatre and Sardi's restaurant. It was a plum deal.

Rehearsals resumed, and what had troubled the creatives about the show in the Florida incarnation could now be fixed before the Broadway opening. Price had wisely stipulated that the previews (the period when the show plays to an audience before the critics arrive) be set at four weeks. Surely this would be ample time to repair, cut, tweak, and excise whatever woes the show had in the Sunshine State. Optimism overflowed. Price was cautious: Florida audiences went easier on shows than New York audiences, but then again so many of the Florida demographic were transplanted upper east coasters and they had demonstrably gone crazy for the show in Florida.

As the show began previews in New York, there was good reason to believe that *Urban Cowboy* had been smiled on by a power no less than in a great Greek tale of transformation and life. What appeared a lost cause and waste of time, talent, and money only so many months earlier was, it seemed, positioned to become a hit.

Broadway unions are a tricky lot, and when a union sneezes Broadway catches a cold. There are three major Broadway unions for those who are active in getting the show itself done daily. The lion of them is the International Alliance of Theatrical Stage Employees (IATSE) which represents Stagehands, Theatrical Stage Employees, Moving Picture Technicians, Artists, and Allied Crafts of the United States, its Territories, and Canada. The Actors' Equity Association (AEA) represents actors and stage managers with some 50,000 U.S. members. The American Federation of Musicians (AFM), which represents the players in Broadway orchestras (and musicians throughout the United States and Canada), is 80,000 strong. Without union membership, no individual is allowed to work as a Broadway employee in one of these capacities.

Broadway producers and the unions can typically settle differences that arise over wages, working conditions, and other contentious matters without much fanfare. Once in a while, however, there is a sticking point that is so sticky that neither side will budge. Such was looming around Broadway about the time that *Urban Cowboy* was setting up shop for previews.

The AFM and the producers were feuding over the minimum number of musicians required to occupy the orchestra pits at each Broadway theatre, a precedent of certain numbers per theatre that had been in place for years and, for a variety of reasons, the producers viewed the old rule as antiquated and no longer necessary. The AFM was fighting, understandably, for the security of its membership and facing daunting, ever-evolving electronic musical instrument technology that could well render their players dispensable. A previous disagreement over the minimum number of musicians that each Broadway theatre must use had been fought out in 1975 during which time Broadway musicals shuttered for 25 days. The result was financial carnage for the artists, for the producer contingency, and for New York City tourism in general. Of course, no one wanted a repeat performance of the mid-1970 debacle, but each side was fighting for their lives and their solvency. A strike deadline was set for Friday, March 7, at 12:01 AM. If a deal was not reached by that time the musicians would walk, but surely and God willing, thought the *Urban Cowboy* team, there would be a resolution.

As the looming hurricane of a strike gathered its footing, *Urban Cowboy* was ratcheting up. In New York City subways, on telephone booths, and omnipresent at the suburban commuter train platforms were unmissable six-foot-tall posters advertising the incoming show. And then there was the coup-de-advertisement: A full page ad in the Sunday *New York Times*, a costly but indispensable method of raising public interest in a soon-to-open show. They say you can tell a lot about a target demographic by the way a product advertises itself, and the *Urban Cowboy* ads boasted a sparkle-toothed, hunky, and bare-chested Matt Cavenaugh riding the infamous Gilley's bull, a shameless portrait of overdone machismo intended to stimulate libidos.

Cavenaugh himself was a newcomer to Broadway, a fresh-faced chiseled-chested actor whose casting was intended as Broadway's parallel to the John Travolta allure of the film. Whether or not he delivered a riveting performance in the show was a secondary concern; *Urban Cowboy* was never intended to present itself as "art," but rather a hoedown of a good time at the theatre, and the show's creators and unpretentious producers never claimed otherwise.

As the show was being fixed up during those early preview days, there was a lurking feeling in the back of everyone's mind that a musicians' strike could potentially throw a lasso around the whole thing. Even a temporary halt in a show's performance playing schedule can send a show to its knees, especially a show trying to find an audience, and trying to find an audience it was. Attendance thus far was devastatingly low.

The Broadhurst Theatre had a potential capacity of just over 9,000 audience members in a week's time, with eight performances each week. The actual number of attendees during the first two weeks was a fraction of that potential number. There was a slight climb in attendance numbers as the previews advanced, but never more than about 3,000 attendees a week. That was only one-third of a house, although it should be noted that, over the four weeks, the show played only 26 of a potential 32-performance schedule. Regardless, there was reason to worry. But if the word of mouth, possibly the theatre's greatest advertising tool, was out and positive then the show could, in theory, build an audience. It was dicey, but it had been done before.

In order to assure that the show would not be halted by a musicians' strike should one occur, Broadway producers were taking matters into their own hands. Some lined up nonunion musicians willing to cross the picket line for a Broadway credit (never mind a shamefaced one) to accompany the show on sophisticated musical computer programs known as "Virtual Orchestras," synthesizer keyboards, and ordinary pianos. Other shows made tapes of the show's music to be played as a substitute for the live musicians. Some shows, especially those with hefty advance sales, would persevere and survive the absence of musicians. Others, like *Urban Cowboy*, would suffer immeasurably without the hard-playing and heavy-strumming band backing the show, which was a fundamental part of the experience.

The producers of *Urban Cowboy*, with the mindset that an ounce of prevention was well worth a pound of cure, opted to go the distance and send the entire musical score to Texas to be recorded in a studio by a professional band. The endeavor would turn out to be expensive, time-consuming, and ultimately just shy of fatal.

There was no resolution to the union and producers' stalemate, and at 12:01 AM on Friday, March 7, 2003, the musicians would go on strike. Three hundred twenty-five Broadway musicians from 17 Broadway musicals were instructed not to show up for the following evening's performances. The contingency plan of using prerecorded tracks at *Urban Cowboy* went into effect. Jed Bernstein, president of the Broadway League, said in a statement: "Broadway is under attack by 325 people."

But the situation went from worse to catastrophic. Show producers received calls around the six o'clock hour on Friday evening, the first day of the strike. The frenzied voice on the other end instructed the producers to come down to the office of the League of American Theatres and Producers, now known as the Broadway League. There, the *Urban Cowboy* producers' worst fear was realized: In solidarity, the other two principal unions would honor the musicians' strike and refuse to perform. A statement released by the president of Actors' Equity read in part: [All 650 members of Equity currently in Broadway shows] "made it clear that they do not wish to perform with virtual orchestras."

Urban Cowboy producers had now spent 100,000 dollars to record the show that wouldn't be performed and lost precious rehearsal time where proactive changes to the show could have been implemented in order to acclimate the actors to performing with the recorded tracks. And now a third gunshot landed right to the head: A darkened theatre until further notice, potentially hundreds of thousands in lost ticket revenue, and worse, no chance for audiences to see the show and then tell their friends. It was as though the other shoe that possibly should have dropped after the workshop had at last plopped to the floor with an ear-splitting thud that could be heard all the way over to 10th Avenue. The Broadway success of *Urban Cowboy* felt like dry tinder awaiting a match.

There was nothing to do but wait. With no actors, Price's hands were tied; but he had risen to meet the ubiquitous challenges of this show before. With few to no options, the creatives and the producers waited for a green light signal that the union and producer standoff had been resolved. Eventually, the AFM blinked and settled for lower house minimums, although both sides claimed to have left with the advantages. Live music was saved in New York theatres for now, but not before the mayor of New York intervened and forced sides to hold all-night negotiating sessions. As of Tuesday, March 11, 2003, Broadway performers, musicians, and stagehands were told to get back on the job. For *Urban Cowboy* the mess looked over.

But it was just the beginning.

"The difference in reaction from Florida to New York was frightening," said Price. The preview audiences were snubbing the show and, as the saying goes in the theatre, they were "staying away in droves." Ever resilient, the producers carried on, hoping against hope that sufficient word of mouth would generate a following. The show was great fun, after all, and, in a burgeoning era of the so-called-jukebox musical, who wouldn't love to have a hoedown of a good time? *Urban Cowboy* was unlike any show on Broadway, after all. And the Florida audiences couldn't have been wrong.

Could they? Maybe not. Maybe so. No one really knew.

As a refreshing spring sun set on the island of Manhattan that March day in 2003, the *Urban Cowboy* Broadway opening ritual was not unlike so many before it. An abundance of flowers flooded the stage door as family and friends of the performers sent best wishes for a long and steady run of the musical. The sentiments were appreciated, although the exuberance the cast and creatives had felt in Florida had drained from their faces some weeks ago. Attendance at the previews had ebbed and flowed. There were whoops and hollers coming from the house of the Broadhurst all the while, but they were but a small contingent. In fact, the numbers, those so far, added up to a doomsday scenario. Even if the reviews weren't solid, so they thought, other shows in recent memory had shouldered eschewing from the critics. *Thoroughly Modern Millie* was playing a block away and had taken a beating from the press, the *New York Times* in particular, and had survived the potential massacre by strong word of mouth.

The strike had put development of the show so far behind that the show wasn't a "whole" finished product until just a day before the first critic attended. Typically, Broadway critics arrive to view the show in the last few previews; by then the show is "frozen," a term that means no more changes are allowed. The critics then depart to their offices and write about their responses, which hit print on the day of the official opening. *Urban Cowboy* barely had time to put the finishing shine on its boots before the reviewers were in attendance.

But another blow had been dealt. In the week prior to the *Urban Cowboy* opening, the United States had declared that the anticipated war against Iraq had begun. The television coverage of the event was expectedly pervasive and constant, so much so that networks repeatedly preempted television commercials. The ads were a lifeline for *Urban Cowboy* and, if the ads weren't running, the show's chances of doing the same grew infinitesimally smaller with each missed advertising opportunity.

With the dismal and disappointing audience reactions to the show being what they were and the latest spate of bad timing, the show's penultimate hope was that somehow the critics would resuscitate the show and generate ticket sales. Short of favorable reviews, perhaps the word-of-mouth angel would descend. If this could be achieved then perhaps the show could run for a bit of time and even potentially squeak out a Tony Award nomination or two and with any luck gain a coveted spot on the Tony telecast, a boon to any show, especially the struggling ones. The chances were meager, but maybe the little engine had some get-up-and-go still in there. But for now the first line of defense was the critics; God willing they like the show.

They didn't. The reviews were blistering and took frequent aim at the show's construct: "The songs in *Urban Cowboy* are a hodgepodge of offerings, some from the film, some written specifically for the show, and some assembled from still other songwriters, with almost all used haphazardly and devoid of dramatic value" (Matthew Murray, *Talkin' Broadway*, March 27, 2003).

This might have been expected given the catch-as-catch-can nature of the development process but some critics dug their claws in much deeper, also taking swipes at the show's "lewd and lascivious" disposition: "*Urban Cowboy* the musical, which opened last night at the Broadhurst Theatre in a conclusive demonstration that it's possible to be vulgar and bland at the same time" (Ben Brantley, *New York Times*, March 28, 2003).

Brantley went on:

> It exudes the mechanical air of a show dutifully assembled according to a low and specific assessment of audience expectations. The jokes are sub-sitcom.

The songs are mostly delivered in a shiny, anonymous twang that might be heard in a Texas-themed pavilion in Disney World.

David Finkle chimed in on the content as well, complaining of the show's "sameness." "For the most part, however, here's a musical that sounds as if a roomful of composers and lyricists got together to write one long, loud, neo-Nashville country song meant to be interrupted as infrequently as possible by dialogue" (*TheatreMania*, March 28, 2003).

Only Clive Barnes of the *New York Post* offered some modest praise of the show, calling it "surprisingly enjoyable," but there was currency therein: The press department at *Urban Cowboy* could use some of his words for advertising purposes.

Choreographer Melinda Roy became, ironically, the scapegoat for much of what the public and critics found unappetizing about the show, criticizing the overuse of the Western-style dancing and faulting the choreography as it did the music with the same syndrome of sameness. In truth, however, it was Roy's choreography that likely salvaged much of the show. The original song material was very good but supported a storyline that was blade-thin and often cliché-vulgar; so when there was a hole in the narrative, there was not much else to do but dance. But if it was diagnosed as indistinguishable and interchangeable from number to number, it did boast a toe-heeling good time through it all. The Tony Awards Nominating Committee thought so too, granting Roy a Best Choreography nomination, although it was widely believed that Twyla Tharp had a lock on the win that year (she did).

The reviews were unfavorable to be sure, and even if New York critics didn't wield the power they once had to assure the run or the closing of a show, building an audience through word of mouth took time and money to keep the show open while doing so. And the producers didn't have it; they had depleted the reserve funds, recording the studio tracks in the event of a musicians' strike and paying for lost rehearsal time. Left with no money, few people in the seats, and theatre parties pulling out and requesting refunds after the reviews were out, a closing notice was posted. Twenty-four hours after the *Urban Cowboy* cast had arrived at the theatre and been greeted by effusive well wishes for prosperity, high spirits, and a bounty of spring bouquets that lined the dressing room tables and window sills, they learned the show's fate. The flowers would be going home with the cast along with the bitter pill of closing and being out of work again in two days' time. The show would close that very weekend.

Urban Cowboy producer Chase Mishkin was exhausted and nearly undone but stoic. She reported to the press that "There are no tourists right now," citing the show which was largely meant to entertain the visitors to New York and, with the war with Iraq in progress, they were now staying home. The show's producers would later have more choice words for New York critics, but for now played it cool.

But the show would be snatched from the clutch of death once more. Producers called friends and raised contingency money to keep the lights on for a few more weeks. Director Price found out as he was preparing to walk from the audience to the stage at the final curtain call of what would be the last performance. Price announced from the stage that the show would continue and "there was pandemonium," he later reported. The public relations machine kicked into overdrive, and the cast went to bed that night knowing that the little engine of a show that could still could.

Peter Marks of the *Washington Post*, never one to soft-pedal his feelings, published a story the following week:

> Nowadays there's a reluctance among Broadway producers to pull an expensive show off life support, no matter how vicious the pains or how long the odds for survival. Take the latest Broadway basket case: *Urban Cowboy* ... opened March 27 to the kind of reviews that can have investors chasing their martinis with Pepto-Bismol.
>
> Washington Post, *April 16, 2003*

But the effort ultimately went south and after a few weeks of limping along with shrinking attendance numbers and dollars, the show packed up and quietly rode away.

Aaron Lathan's title for the *Esquire* article on which the film and Broadway musical were based was "The Ballad of the Urban Cowboy: America's Search for True Grit." Looking back at *Urban Cowboy* as it transitioned mediums, the narrative of the story may have been limp but the grit of the creatives and the producers to get the show into the Main Stem argued that *Urban Cowboy* was never intended to shine as high art, only as a good time. The *Mamma Mia* model proved that the objective was viable, certainly in the time period following September 11, 2001, when audiences might be looking to feel lighter. This all may have been rational thinking, but due to just too many goblins flying in the face of good intentions, success wasn't possible.

Was *Urban Cowboy* flawed? Most certainly it was handicapped by too many country-pop songs commenting second hand on the narrative instead of driving it forward in a conventional moment-to-moment fashion. And surely director Price must have felt as though he was constantly pushing out from a corner to achieve a vision that he hadn't himself conceived but was saddled with retrofitting to resemble a traditional musical theatre piece. Nevertheless, the show was punch-drunk with good times, and there was much to celebrate. The real question concerned whether *Urban Cowboy* was itself an unfortunate victim of circumstances.

Oh, remember that hoedown–showdown rift over the girl between Bud and the convict? It came to a head in the second act via that mechanical bull ride. Bud prevailed and it rained money. If only *Urban Cowboy* the musical had enjoyed the same fate.

4

THE PIRATE QUEEN

Opened April 25, 2007
Closed June 17, 2007

Tell a story that captivates your audience.

Key dramatis personae

Frank Galati, Director: Well-seasoned and well-intentioned, Galati had helmed large-scale musicals with gusto.

Graciela Daniele, Musical Staging: Fiery and able, this Broadway power-house brought the invaluable sustenance of a woman's perspective to *The Pirate Queen*.

Alain Boublil, Claude-Michel Schönberg, Richard Maltby, Jr., and John Dempsey, Music, Lyrics, and Book: Formidable, to say the least, these collaborators had a string of hits behind them, including *Les Misérables* and *Miss Saigon*.

Mark Dendy, Choreography: Officially credited with "additional choreography," Dendy was replaced with Daniele prior to the New York opening.

Moya Doherty and John McColgan, Lead Producers: The husband and wife brain-parents of the *Riverdance* empire, they assembled a "dream team" of creators and designers.

When a pop culture throwback appears earnestly unaware of how firmly its style and conception are rooted in another era, is it retro or just out-moded? The lumbering epic "The Pirate Queen" comes down on the latter side. As *Les Misérables* creators Alain Boublil and Claude-Michel Schönberg showed with their last excursion into romantically embroidered 16th century historical tapestry, the commercially ill-fated *Martin Guerre*, the French composing team's bombastic 1980s megamusical formula now sits stodgily onstage. Their all-plot, no heart new show is persuasively sung by a valiant cast, yet it never forges an emotional connection with the audience.

David Rooney, Variety, *April 5, 2007*

The Pirate Queen

Spring 2007

New York City

Oh, beauty, there you were all dressed up but going nowhere, really. The optics were magnificent, though. That backdrop of a glittering, stately azure and ruby-red sky that doted over the gracious 16th-century coastal waters of Ireland packed a real visual wallop. And when the full fury of an ocean tempest was unleashed and then hovered over a hand-to-hand battle of blinding swords (and unmovable wills) the effect was awe-inspiring. The costumes depicting the Elizabethan court with Elizabeth herself adorned in ornate royal guise, embellished with ruff and whisk, were candy to the eye. And the dancing was equally inspired; the show's producers were the co-creators and producers of the well-traveled *Riverdance* theatrical properties who knew how a crowd-pleaser was built.

The show's pedigree was evident, and the creative team had enough world-wide awards and accolades between them to sink a ship. Some say they ultimately did. Director Frank Galati had helmed *Ragtime*, which was universally praised and awarded, and his *The Grapes of Wrath* adaptation was lauded near and far as revelatory. Graciela Daniele, theatrical royalty since a quarter century prior, was credited with the musical staging of the show. Claude-Michel Schönberg and Alain Boublil, the show's composer and principal lyricist, had also written *Les Misérables*, which racked up thousands of performances in the Broadway and West End runs and thousands more worldwide and is one of the world's most known musicals. The two were also the writing team that created *Miss Saigon*, another show that played nearly 10 years on Broadway and the West End, smashing box office records. Between this esteemed creative team and Irish dance choreographer Carol Leavy Joyce, there was nary a link that wasn't as sure-footed as the show's magnificent dancing itself. The producers of the show had fashioned it that way in unanimous agreement that if there ever was a hit-maker dream team of a Broadway-bound musical, this was one. But even the almighty-est of theatremakers are impossibly pressed to turn stagnant subject matter to gold or persuade an audience to care when there is little about the material to invest in or it feels hopelessly yawn-ish. Eventually the latter, probably above all else, was *The Pirate Queen*'s most glaring fatal flaw, as David Rooney eventually would point out in his *Variety* review. The audience barely connected.

This is not to imply that the story of *The Pirate Queen* isn't compelling. Based on the novel *Grania: She-King of the Irish Seas* by Morgan Llewelyn, the narrative wasn't uninteresting as much as it was faint and distant. There were overarching themes that bridged gaps like girl power, love triumphant, precipitous forward-generational change, and common ground among adversaries, but these were all couched within a storyline that often generated only a certain blank apathy from the other side of the footlights.

Grace (Gráinne) O'Malley is the daughter of Dubhdara, the Chieftain of the Irish O'Malley clan, a 16th-century seafaring tribe that punishes the English, who annexed Ireland, by robbing English treasure ships off Clew Bay and absconding with the loot.

Grace has been in love with Tiernan, a young sailor, since childhood but women are naturally not allowed to sail with the men as they take their sea excursions. Today a new ship is to be christened and before the crew sails there is a celebration. As the women are ushered from the ship prior to sailing, Grace tells her father that she would like to sail with the crew. Dubhdara declares this impossible, as women aboard the ship are thought to be a bad omen and a distraction for the men. Grace implores him with a full-throated ballad early in the show about "chained" women who wish to "sail unrestrained" but her father will not relent.

The show played early performances in Chicago after rehearsing in New York in the summer of 2006, and the Chicago reviews of the show were tepid, blaming murky storytelling and ill-defined, skinny characterizations. The above-mentioned song was a New York add-on to clarify Grace's disposition and introduce her trajectory. But even before the early reviews were in print in the windy city, Internet Broadway chat boards lit up with complaints that the Chicago iteration was humdrum and the topical matter not vivid enough to carry a full-length musical. But this wasn't terribly unusual for a show out of town, and the show would shut down for a spell after the Chicago run prior to resuming rehearsals in New York in order for the creative team to work on the revisions before opening on Broadway.

Internally, despite the unenthusiastic Chicago critical reception, one cast member remarked,

> The cast was fairly optimistic although we didn't necessarily disagree with the [Chicago] reviews. [However], I had a memorable session of drinks with some of the NYC crew while in Chicago and they were not nearly as kind about our prospects.

Nevertheless, so they thought, if any production could be turned around, this one could. The cast member said,

> The cast was amazingly talented, the design work was gorgeous and Frank Galati, Mark Dendy, Graciela Daniele, and the *Riverdance* producers were all at the height of their careers. We also had Boublil and Schönberg as the writers whose previous successes made them seem invincible.

History champions the notion that the chronicles of musical theatre history are littered with musicals that were rife with problems out of town but with revisions found their way. Naturally there are those, plenty of them, that couldn't recover and came into the Main Stem a stinker. *The Pirate Queen* wouldn't fall on that side of history, or so everyone held out hope; but Galati, even-tempered, systematic, and meticulous, must have been feeling the pinch of being hamstrung by a less-than-interesting musical by this point.

There were other problems early on:

"Suddenly there it [the show] was, fully realized onstage with its 42-member cast and extravagant sets and costumes. The question I asked myself," Ms. Doherty said, "was where did the power of that music go?" "I knew it was there but we had lost touch with it," said producer Maya Doherty in a *New York Times* interview.

But again, the experience she describes is hardly rare as a show transitions from the rehearsal room to the stage. A rehearsal room, intimate and barren, is an organic, controlled habitat. There are few distractions; the story spins from a cellular level outward and once airborne is received by compassionate receptors—the show family. In the physical theatre the show becomes more vulnerable. The intimacy of relationships is challenged by the new cavernous space and has given way temporarily to an assembly of pragmatic challenges. Costumes, marks to hit, volume levels, pacing, backstage collaboration, and so on now subvert, if only for a while, the kind of stark simplicity that the rehearsal room offers. *The Pirate Queen* had, it seemed, come down with that age-old syndrome, a semi-terrible case of "the show is really big."

But the illness had spread beyond a certain purity that had given way to behemoth production elements. There was considerable confusion from the audience about who was doing what to whom and why and who that person was anyway. There was even greater concern that the leading character was registering with the audience with sluggish uncertainty rather than as the commanding proto-feminist the creators had intentioned.

Richard Maltby Jr. was credited as co-lyricist and as providing "additional material" for *Miss Saigon* and saw *The Pirate Queen* in Chicago, reliving a role he had played before and delivering a succinct list of necessary fixes to the creators. The view from 30,000 feet is nearly always more clearheaded.

"Seems like old times," Mr. Maltby said in the memo to his former collaborators. He went on to opine a rundown of the problems with the show's storytelling: too much explaining and not enough action; not enough historical context; the dramatic tension that should be present in this or that scene isn't there. "I for some reason feel a personal stake in having this show be a success," Mr. Maltby wrote in his conclusion, "partly because I'm fond of you and Claude-Michel, but it's even more because I think that you have a really great musical here, potentially, if it can just be unlocked and released."

Maltby Jr. was brought later aboard the ship as a clarifier-in-chief, which translates in show business jargon to "show doctor." But his inclusion on the team was not the only change. It was widely agreed that the musical staging needed overhaul, too. Mark Dendy would leave the production and be replaced by Graciela Daniele, with whom Galati had worked on *Ragtime*.

One change that Maltby Jr. and the team agreed upon straightaway that must be made was to raise the stakes for the leading character. Grace's persona, one that might rearrange the moon if she had her druthers, had not touched down for the audience the way that the writers had imagined. The trouble was that Grace's irrepressible rebel spirit did not, some complained, fully register until much too late and even then fell to the side of more tepid and less white-hot. With the inclusion now of a newly minted song entitled "Woman," Grace was framed fittingly.

The tide is high and Grace takes matters into her own hands, disguising herself as a boy and stowing away on the ship as it sails, to which the men are none the wiser. The newly minted ship is hardly out of port when a ferocious storm steamrolls toward it. As the tempest batters the ship, a sail snags and Grace volunteers to climb and cross hand-over-hand, reaching the sail and liberating it. The men of the ship applaud and delight in the young "boy's" bravery. Dubhdara is astonished but not surprised to reveal the young boy's true identity. Furious as he is that Grace has deceived him and the crew, he allows her to remain on the ship until the voyage is complete. Tiernan is elated that Grace will remain and the lovers pledge their hearts to one another although their relationship must remain hushed, "Here on this Night."

Critics and pundits quibbled that too many characters incessantly pledge and vow this or that and too often those promises come couched within bombastic ballads that sound like a throwback to a previous musical theatre generation. "*The Pirate Queen* registers as a relic of a long-gone era, and I don't mean the 1500s," snickered Ben Brantley as to the "bloated" writing style of Boublil and Schönberg. (Lest we forget they rather invented it, or at minimum were complicit in the 1980s when Broadway and the West End caught the fever of musical bluster.) Brantley added that "There's not a ballad or choral number in *The Pirate Queen* that doesn't sound like a garbled echo of a more stirring tune from *Les Miz* …," and these moments seemed just a few of many imbued with the brand of sap that turned too many musical theatre thinkers off in 2007, when New York theatre trends and stylings were literally shrinking.

Soon after, with bangs, rumbles, and dings of percussion and orchestral atonality, the *Pirate Queen* ship is viciously attacked by an English warship. Vigorous swordplay ensues and Dubhdara appears to be out-sworded by his sparring adversary. Naturally, Grace intervenes and triumphs. The rebel Irish have crushed the offending English and a wounded Dubhdara praises Grace: "You saved the ship my daughter, you are truly a warrior," to which Tiernan unhesitatingly adds: "She's more than a warrior captain. She's a leader." Her father proclaims that he will train her to become the ship's captain as the reward for her bravery.

"You are the Pirate Queen," he bestows.

The sequence had looked much different in Chicago but the improved-upon version that appeared later in New York still gave ammunition to those who thought *The Pirate Queen* worked too hard. More than one Chicago writer remarked that the action was poorly realized and too often there was confusion as to who was fighting whom and who was prevailing. With Dendy's departure, Graciela Daniele had been tasked with clarifying the sequences. One strategy toward that end was to empower Grace all the more, supporting her well- and hard-earned "right" to become commander of the vessel. The mission was accomplished but many felt that the sequence and too many like it was gratuitous bombast, in part prompting Brantley to take another swipe in his review:

> The operating theory behind *The Pirate Queen* would appear to be taken from an appropriately ocean-themed bit of zoology: If, like a shark, it never stops moving, then it will stay alive. The optimism is misplaced.

As a pompous brass ripens to a spritely harpsichord (naturally) the scene shifts into the bed chamber of Queen Elizabeth I who has only worn the English crown for a day. Her attendants pitter and skitter about like dizzy schoolgirls, but no one in the audience notices the silliness of it all; they have unwittingly fallen under the spell of the royal costumes which, for the remainder of the evening, will become the de facto star and center of attention in every scene in which they appear.

The couture and overall scale of the physical production gloated grandly, a rare three-dimensional effort among one-dimensional characterizations and writing. The costume department alone was an astounding operation. Martin Pakledinaz and his team designed over 300 costumes that were executed over nine costume shops in New York and elsewhere. Such lengths were gone to to get it right that a firm in London was engaged to replicate centuries-old patterns on original looms. Such was the size of many of the costumes that Queen Elizabeth alone occupied four feet of real estate when onstage.

Having just risen on the morning following her coronation, she huskily orders the lady servants to "Turn your backs!" having vowed to never let anyone see her not dressed in royal guise, fearing that a woman could never be taken seriously as a monarch: "The girl that I once was is dead … and what is here must never be seen," she reasons.

Elizabeth's suspicions prove founded. The men appear to have positioned themselves among themselves to dominate the domestic and foreign affairs of her reign, appeasing her as necessary. After a deferential morning greeting to her majesty, they assure her that all is right and well with a "Rah-Rah, Tip-Top" and "everything's right as rain" except for that recent skirmish in Ireland in which the Englishmen were dominated by the O'Malley clan. And with that, in a demeanor both brittle and snappish, the Queen orders Bingham to squash the Irish rebellion and kill Grace O'Malley.

Across the water, anxiety among Dubhdara and the O'Malley clan swells with the anticipation of English retribution and the ramping up of English aggression. Dubhdara makes overtures to the leader of rival Clan O'Flaherty and proposes that the two clans put aside ancient rivalries and work together to fend off the encroaching English. Uncertain of the proposition, the O'Flaherty chieftain suggests that a marriage be arranged between his son Donal and Grace. Once a son is produced, the consummation of the tribes may then be transacted.

Tiernan looks on as Grace and Donal marry and later, accompanied by the articulations of uilleann pipes and whistles, bellows that when Donal dresses Grace "up in bow ... lavished eternally with flowers ... I'll be there." (Remember that quip about all those pledges and vows?)

In Chicago the creatives discovered that, despite protestations from the producers that *The Pirate Queen* "will not be *Riverdance II*," the Irish dancing was in too short supply, and an extravagant celebration of Irish footwork that had played the world over to sold-out crowds including Broadway couldn't be wrong. Sheepishly, the producers acquiesced and agreed to add it to the work list of changes in New York.

Life isn't all that rosy at the Donal and Grace home and it appears that Grace intends to exercise her option under Irish law to annul the marriage if one or both parties contend that the marriage isn't a suitable one within three years' time. News comes that English troops have landed at Belclare, a town positioned between Clew Bay and Rockfleet, and the men rush off to surround the troops. But soon news comes from the women that the English have now landed in the town and Grace realizes that the landing at Belclare was a diversion. Capturing Grace is the true objective of the English landing; while the men are away at Belclare, English troops will invade the homes of the "helpless women" and seize Grace. With this, Grace rallies the women: "We must now be soldiers!" Again Grace bests an Englishman, this time Bingham himself.

Back in England the costumes are still ravishing. The Queen rails at Sir Bingham for not completing his assigned task. Fearful for his position and his life, he pledges an oath to Elizabeth that he will not fail again and will not fail to deliver Grace's heart to the Queen. Elizabeth delights that Bingham appears to now understand his proper place in the hierarchy, and a humbled and emasculated Bingham exits the stage.

Dubhdara has been mortally wounded in the battle. According to custom, his body is burned on a flaming boat set out to sea as the full company wails "Sail to the Stars!" Flames. Torturous heartbreak. Grace promises to "fight on." The finale of the act has been costly and hard-won. In Chicago, the sequence was a more meager version than the one that anchored in New York. The burning funeral pyre itself was not a terribly tricky ordeal and was hardly given a second thought. But when performances began many remarked that they thought it too looked artificial. Like so much else in multimillion-dollar musicals there is bang in the bling and the sequence was overhauled to look more impressive with a 20,000-dollar price tag attached.

The Pirate Queen, so some of the intermission buzz went, was a thrillingly executed but largely prosaic tale. Even as the musical score was rousing and the physical production exquisite the question that would be answered in time was whether a tank of a show like this could be successful coasting along on those laurels. History shouted loudly that this was indeed not only possible but, in fact, somewhat commonplace in the commercial theatre—give them enough visceral thrills and pure entertainment and the seats tend to be filled, certainly for a while. But to this end *The Pirate Queen* faced the same challenge that so many other shows had grappled with: The Hilton Theatre is itself mammoth at around 1,900 seats and filling them, critical to making enough money to cover the overhead let alone make a profit, is in and of itself a creative and pragmatic challenge.

Dubhdara's deathbed wish is granted as Act II commences. While Grace gives birth below deck, up above the men pace expectantly. Word is handed up that the child is a boy and the men celebrate with whiskey; the child is next in the line of succession to chieftain of the combined clans now that the transaction of the two clans into one has been consummated. Grace gazes at her newborn and there transpires a quantum leap of character. The Grace who had so vociferously thundered for female equality now softly reflects on the essence and exclusivities of being a female.

Grace and Tiernan reunite and another bloated ballad thumps the audience with the reminder that the derivative "mawkish power-ballad" culture remains alive and well. But the formula has been wearing blade-thin all evening and by now has run itself downwind to a tipping point. Naturally some critics pounced, complaining that the stentorian music in theatre was passé as was the era of the mega-musical outmoded by trendy boutique musicals with smaller scales and smaller casts. Not everyone agreed. But it didn't help matters that a scaled-back revival of *Les Misérables* was playing on Broadway just a couple of blocks away and that struck many as commercially greedy and (worse) as dated and unnecessary. Because the alchemy of both *Les Misérables* and *The Pirate Queen* was not dissimilar, naturally there was comparison.

> It really isn't fair to open the poor *Pirate Queen* when a revival of *Les Misérables* is running just two blocks away. Granted, the current *Misérables* is smaller and tinnier than the original (which closed only in 2003). But it plies the same historical-epic formula as *The Pirate Queen* to far more coherent and compelling ends.
>
> *Ben Brantley,* New York Times, *April 5, 2007*

But for whatever annoyances the music generated for the critical jury, the trouble went on. The second act narrative of the show was clotted, dense, and stodgy to the point that one critic argued that the whole show had been "suffocated by plot" and another to quip that the show was "all plot, no heart." It wasn't too far-reaching to agree. The remainder of the second half played much more like an impertinent amalgamation of the musical theatre of a generation past and a sleepy documentary.

Queen Elizabeth contemplates her royal obligation to produce an heir and Sir Bingham jockeys for the post as queen consort. Grace is taken prisoner by the English and held for seven years as Bingham wraps up his conquest of Ireland. Donal is killed and Tiernan vows to take their child under his care. Tiernan offers himself to Queen Elizabeth in exchange for Grace's freedom to which the Queen agrees. Grace returns to a desecrated Ireland then sails back to England on The Pirate Queen and meets woman-to-woman, face-to-face with Queen Elizabeth, both women of starkly dissimilar backgrounds who had striking parallels between them.

The meeting sequence was problematic, but Galati was in a precarious spot. Because little is known of the actual content of the meeting between the two "queens," it would have been presumptuous to have represented the scene out loud. Rather, Galati wisely elected to place the two behind a screen only to again emerge once a resolution has been achieved. Of course, this registered with many critics as anticlimactic and gave their criticisms oxygen.

The Pirate Queen opened on Broadway to dreadful reviews in spite of the over-haul after the Chicago tryout. The changes, however, despite weeks in the rehearsal room post-Chicago to clarify the storytelling and tidy and expand the physical production, didn't make much difference to the public and critical responses. If Chicago audiences were likely to be more lenient on the out-of-town tryout, choosing to mostly dwell on the positive (the physical production and visceral thrills therein) and be quick to point out that although far from perfect the show could be fixed, then the New York critics head straight for the jugular with quips like "*Pirate* should walk the plank." It went on from there. Clive Barnes of the *New York Post* complained that the score was "repetitive and self-congratulatory" with "banal lyrics."

The opening night party on Union Square in Manhattan was a dazzler replete with a surprise appearance by actor Gabriel Byrne. Hoping to spread the word and perhaps rejuvenate the theatregoing public's appetite for the "epic" musical, a trend that had been tamped down by the "boutique" musical infatuation of late, the producers hired Byrne to host a costly television special called "The Making of *The Pirate Queen*" which debuted nearly simultaneously with the Broadway opening.

But as the reviews rolled in, the mood darkened over the course of that unusually blustery early April night. Maybe it didn't matter. Many of Broadway's longest-running musicals had survived an onslaught of negative critical responses. As we know by now, some shows seem bulletproof and impervious to a critic's pen.

But the "go big or go home" maxim the producers adopted was a crap shoot. A big box office intake was crucial in order to keep the show afloat at a sky-high weekly operating expense (often referred to in theatre parlance as "the nut") which is the amount of money required to pay the bills. This is to say nothing of the initial cost to produce the show. In the case of *The Pirate Queen*, the latter figure was upward of 16 million dollars. Epic musical theatre indeed.

The cast had seen the writing on the wall for some time and feared that the show's days were numbered. "Once we were in previews in NYC and they (the creatives) stopped trying to make any changes, it became pretty clear that things were not salvageable. Those were some sad days," said a cast member.

Momentarily encouraged after the New York opening, *The Pirate Queen* producers noted that the show had a fair degree of advance (tickets that had been purchased before the critics had registered their responses) and that in the week following the reviews the ticket sales were up by 8 percent. Yes, maybe it didn't matter. *The Pirate Queen* was epic even in the face of the show's seeming inability to forge a relationship with its audience. Surely the grandeur and a show that could boast "from the creators of *Les Misérables* and *Miss Saigon*" would stand a chance, if only long enough to gather a following to become a tourist magnet.

But *The Pirate Queen*, like so many others, was eventually hoisted by its own petard. The show was so expensive to produce and run that it required a huge number of seats to be filled to pay the bills and without a "star," reviews that ranged from unenthusiastic to disastrous, and without a healthy presale, the situation was dire and increasingly grim.

Cast members had another take. A cast member said,

> There was a pretty strong feeling that we were being shut out (certainly in terms of Tony Noms—we had none) because the producers were Broadway outsiders and not from the U.S. Another element to our untimely demise had to do with Mel Brooks wanting the theatre for *Young Frankenstein*. There were pretty strong indications that the theatre owners were dealing with Brooks on the side and forced us out earlier than they may have needed.

The hammer came down after only 85 regular performances of *The Pirate Queen*, a show that had arrived with all that ballyhoo too soon traded at a discount and quietly shuttered, losing its entire investment. There was talk initially, as there so often is, of another life for the show elsewhere but the talk never materialized to much. Perhaps the era of the epic musical had passed. Maybe ticket buyers still keen to hear overwrought ballads situated within mega shows optioned the revival of *Les Misérables* playing down the street. Maybe historical drama was passé and outdated. Whatever the reason for its demise, *The Pirate Queen* will fall from the pages of musical theatre history as a show that got so much wrong yet so much right at the wrong time.

5

ROCKY

Opened March 13, 2014
Closed August 17, 2014

Sometimes it's all in the timing (and the tourists).

Key dramatis personae

Alex Timbers, Director: Crafty and intrepid, he directed the Broadway productions of *Bloody Andrew Jackson* and *Peter and the Starcatcher*.

Kelly Devine, Choreographer *Rock of Ages*, *Doctor Zhivago*, and Steven Hoggett, Choreographer *The Light Princess*, *The Curious Incident of the Dog in the Night-Time*, worked on *Rocky* in such an interchangeable way that at no time in recent memory can one recall fight and dance choreography being more inexorably or inevitably linked.

Lynn Ahrens and Stephen Flaherty, Lyrics and Music: With two of the smartest pens in the business, the team has written a handful of marvelous and memorable scores. The team won the Tony Award for *Ragtime*.

Thomas Meehan, Book Writer: Tony Award–winning consummate heart-tugger and funny man, his scripts include a number of musical theatre classics including the scripts for *Annie*, *Hairspray*, and *The Producers*.

Sylvester Stallone, Book Writer and Co-Producer: Hollywood icon of the *Rocky* film franchises as writer/actor.

Stage Entertainment, Producer: German mega presenters turned producers responsible for both the Hamburg and Broadway productions.

The official curtain time for *Rocky,* the new musical at the Winter Garden Theater, is 8 on most nights. But at the risk of promoting tardiness among theatergoers, I feel obligated to point out that the show doesn't really get started until 10:10 or thereabouts.

That's when a production that has seemed to be down for the count since the opening bars of its overture suddenly acquires a pulse. And the audience wakes out of a couch potato stupor—the kind you experience when you have the television tuned to an infomercial station—to the startling tingle of adrenaline in its blood. Of course, by that point, it's all over but the fighting.

Ben Brantley, New York Times *Review, March 13, 2014*

Rocky

Yo, Sylvester Stallone, for god's sake don't say that! Don't you know that it's terrible luck in the theatre to announce that your show is "going to be a big hit" before it's even been produced?

Sheesh.

"I really truly believe that this thing here is going to be extraordinarily successful. I don't know how it can fail because it's about the people," the Hollywood actor and writer and star of the *Rocky* film franchise told Sky News. Well, no, Mr. Stallone, with all due respect, it's actually "about" placing asses in seats and to do that a show must generate a certain universal appeal, which *Rocky,* the Broadway musical, ultimately didn't do on Broadway.

It is arguable that the so-called "tired businessman" era of the 1950s and beyond would have made, or did make, musicals involving sports into an easier ticket sale. There are several compelling points to support the theory, however. Easy air travel made trips to New York for business meetings much more commonplace. If one presupposes that the likelihood that those travelers were (certainly) nearly exclusively male and (likely) mostly White, it stands to reason that sports musicals would appeal to this generalized demographic of visitor dollars. Moreover, if most of these fellas were on expense accounts and ticket prices were exponentially cheaper in those days, ticket buyers could afford to be less fussy as to how to spend those discretionary expense account funds.

Now for a moment let us presuppose, for the sake of argument, that today most Broadway tickets are sold to attendees from the New York metro area who, like in the old days, represented the majority of the audience and attended as frequently as they once did. Then let's assume that deciding how those dollars would be spent (e.g., which show to see) was for the most part decided by males. Then let's presuppose that most of the attendees were, in fact, males who might well want to see a show revolving around sports, namely boxing.

Were any one of these true then *Rocky* might have found the kind of support that would have put the, well, asses in the seats.

But statistics provided by the Broadway League in the 2016–2017 annual demographics report belie the above. The report identifies its mission by stating that it seeks to compare(s) current Broadway habits in New York City to previous seasons and aids in predicting trends for the future. This report is the 20th publication in a longitudinal study that tracks the trends and changes of the Broadway audiences over time.

The report found that while the number of ticket buyers who were from the New York area was the highest in years, tourists bought approximately 61 percent of the tickets to Broadway shows. Of those, approximately 66 percent were females, and of those, 51 percent of female respondents said they made the purchasing decision to see a show compared to 44 percent of male respondents.

These facts alone could take a musical like *Rocky* down for the count.

The show did stand a chance with fans of the film (that won an Oscar in 1977 for Best Picture) but that margin was thin, certainly when over 10,000 seats needed to be filled weekly.

So Rocky, and Saint Anthony pray for us now, we barely knew you before you were forced to hang up your gloves, which is too bad for us because your creators and designers made you into one hell of a good musical.

Rocky the film was a post-Vietnam hit whose popularity was bolstered by the great wave of 1976 Bicentennial nationalism that at one level served as a healing process for the country. The ravages of the Vietnam War, as well as the tearing apart of generations and the Watergate scandal, left in their aftermath a country confused, distrustful, and shouldering something of an identity crisis. The *Rocky* story was a metaphor for the history of the United States itself with all the right dramatic components that stirred patriotism: The underdog that in the American Revolutionary War fought "from the heart" and whipped the great adversary through brute and willpower, lost and disenfranchised characters on the cusp of society that find their way, and in more recent times, a country that got beat up pretty badly but at least its "nose ain't broke."

Having thought for years that *Rocky* would make a compelling musical, Stallone, who was the rights holder to the story, approached Thomas Meehan about a possible stage adaptation. Meehan's star had begun to shine ever brighter in the early 2000s having adapted Mel Brooks' *The Producers* for the stage and before that, among others, Meehan had written the script for that chestnut named *Annie*. The other components of the writing team were also gold standard worthy. Lynn Ahrens and Stephen Flaherty had written, among others, *My Favorite Year, Lucky Stiff, Dessa Rose, A Man of No Importance*, and *Ragtime*, but only the latter, a towering example of both potent storytelling and regal theatricality, stacked up as a hit, although all had sterling scores. *Seussical* had a respectable Broadway run but has mostly seen its success in regional theatre and a smartly conceived truncated adaptation.

In the 1990s, *Ragtime* was brought to life in a fashion that was at that time a less-traveled road to Broadway. Of course, as discussed elsewhere in this volume, earlier generations of Broadway musicals might typically rehearse in New York City and then travel "out of town" to one of several usual cities to "try out" (read: fix what is not working). Boston, Philadelphia, and New Haven were all destinations that in those days were far enough away from New York to avoid "prying eyes" and allow the shows to "get it right." As far off as Detroit and beyond the show would play nightly in front of an audience and the creative team could assess the shortcomings, write and rewrite fixes, and implement those in daytime rehearsals prior to that evening's performance.

Over time as musicals became much larger and stage technology advanced, pre-Broadway travel became more complex and therefore less practical. The old pre-Broadway tryout didn't make as much sense as developing the shows to get them right at regional theatres and then gradually mounting them in New York as bug-free as could be, sometimes after runs and development in as many as several regional houses. In the 1970s, the idea of the "workshop" was introduced (the idea had been around for decades but that generation congealed the idea) and this concept allowed shows to somewhat organically develop in rehearsal rooms before being mounted in earnest for a "presentation" for audience consumption, often in an attempt to persuade money backers to put up bucks to finance the whole shebang.

In the current generation of Broadway musicals, a number of options exist for pre-Broadway development. Disney's *Frozen* held both a "developmental lab" and a "workshop" prior to traveling the show to Denver to get the kinks out, which was not an unusual course. Other shows like *Spider-Man: Turn Off the Dark* and *King Kong* (both discussed in this volume) were simply too bulky and, therefore, too costly to travel and optioned to head right to a Gotham stage.

Other shows like *Ragtime* developed out of town as produced by Canadian impresario Garth Drabinsky who, having acquired the live theatrical division of a Canadian entertainment conglomerate, agreed to produce the show locally prior to the American premiere. Lynn Ahrens noted that she found the Toronto experience very positive, whereas when developing *Seussical* in Boston some years later "[i]t felt like you were standing there in your underwear trying to do the show" ostensibly because there were eyes everywhere reporting what shaky ground the show was teetering on. To exacerbate the state of unrest, it appeared that someone within the company was sending out daily tattletale emails to bigmouthed theatre folks reporting on who was fighting with whom within the show over the changes and anything else. This, of course, created a ruckus of anticipation of a whopper of a mess, and by the time the show got to New York it already had a black eye and a "reputation." One seasoned theatregoer remarked, "It could have been the best show since *My Fair Lady* and I still wouldn't have seen it the same way with all the bad news that arrived in (New York) before the show did."

But out-of-town engagements are a "damned if you do but also damned if you don't" situation. To revise and revise until a show meets lofty New York expectations the show must play in front of an audience, yet these days word gets out about the condition of the show out of town instantaneously and if things aren't going well. Reflecting on the dilemma, one Broadway producer lamented, "There's really not as much of a protective environment any more to develop a show out of town because anyone can tweet or send an email and snap a photo."

So when German theatrical titan Stage Entertainment, a Hamburg-based subsidiary of Stage Holdings Ltd., offered to produce *Rocky*, there was a sigh of relief within the camp of the musical; a German production would place some appreciated space between the musical and New York where everyone, it seemed, had an opinion. Stage Holdings Ltd. had been a licensor of musicals, mounting mostly American megahit musicals and translating them into German, but had more recently developed new musicals for international markets. The company reached deeply into its considerably deep pockets and spent 20 million dollars to produce the world premiere of *Rocky* the musical, a striking contrast to the shoestring budget of the 1975 film that paid back 117 million in domestic box office alone.

German press lauded the show as a "triumph" and the production team was itself celebrated as a revelation. The Hamburg box office was strong and steady. A Broadway run seemed sure but some worried about the question of Broadway success because of tastes in cultural crossovers. German audiences hadn't devoured *Les Misérables*, for example, the way that American audiences had and American audiences had laughed *Dance of the Vampires* into a quick Broadway demise. Other crossover shows in one direction were more universally embraced but some, especially those intended for grown-up consumption and having unorthodox subject matter for a commercial Broadway musical, were dark horses. *Rocky* seemed to fall into these criteria quite naturally. It was an uneasy feeling but the show pressed forward.

"At the time when I got the offer (to do the show in New York) I was shopping to buy an apartment and I had thought I hit my top end price point," said one production member.

> When the offer to do the show came I thought about revising that price point up because, hey, I had a Broadway show and (if the show ran) I could afford it. Then I worried about if the show would run because of what it was. I went and walked the TKTS line (the half-price ticket line in Times Square) one Friday to see how many of those people looked like they'd buy tickets to *Rocky*. What I saw was mostly families and older ladies in pairs and trios buying tickets to *Mamma Mia* and *Phantom*. Almost no one looked like they'd jump to buy a ticket to a show about a boxer. I kept my apartment buying price point on the lower end.

The sentiment wasn't unusual or surprising. Check writers were still taking less risk and exercising more caution since the devastation of the 2008 U.S. banking crisis. Investable income, even from many of the most reliable "angels," was still in "flight to safety" mode having been burned by investments that tanked in the wake.

And the problems didn't stop there. Where cautious investors exist, so do skittish ticket buyers, and where investors could "write off" a bomb show on their tax statements, disappointed patrons who bought tickets were left with little by way of the experience. Accordingly, it is little wonder that *Mamma Mia*, *Phantom*, and a host of other shows on Broadway in those days were still holding court as "sure things," which in this context means "won't disappoint."

But *Rocky* appeared to be in safe stead on the money-raising side. Joop van den Ende, the European mogul impresario behind the Hamburg *Rocky* and so many other German hits, had a long list of reliable moneymen and moneywomen on both sides of the Atlantic who, one theatre insider noted, were quite "bullish" on the project, certainly after noting the healthy balance sheet and favorable reviews in Hamburg, where the show was still running. The Broadway version budget was reportedly set at around 16.5 million dollars and a reported one-quarter of that was said to be budgeted for the set alone, which included a regulation-size boxing ring that rose and moved out and over the "Golden Circle" of theatre seats for which patrons had laid out a hefty premium to vacate at the finale of the show in order to take their places in bleachers on the stage itself. Somewhere in Heaven or Hell, the long-dead scoundrel impresario David Merrick was giving an approving thumbs-up at the gimmick.

Sylvester Stallone and cohorts, the producers of the 1975 film, got sweetheart deals in the contractual arrangements. According to the *New York Post*, a massive payout of 600,000 dollars was reportedly paid for the rights to tell the story, which is usually closer to around 100,000 dollars in similar deals. They also signed on for an 8,000-dollar-a-week payout until the show was paid off and then would convert to a 1 percent take of the box office gross. But their special kitty didn't stop there. They were also entitled to 20 percent of the net, according to the *Post*. With all this, one wonders if there would be anything left over to keep the theatre ushers around.

Andy Karl had played the boxer in the workshop version outing of the show and was handed off the title role on Broadway from Drew Sarich who played the prizefighter in Germany. Director Alex Timbers, choreographer Kelly Devine, and fight choreographer Steven Hoggett all repeated their Hamburg assignments in New York.

Understanding that the theme song from the *Rocky* film was so incontrovertibly associated with the product, the musical adopted it and it opened the show. As the house lights dimmed, "Gonna Fly Now" was trumpeted at ear-splitting decibel levels over the speakers as if to assure the audience that this stage version of *Rocky* would come close enough to the beloved original film that it would set neophyte or casual theatregoers familiar with the film version at ease. Whether the choice was intended to accomplish that isn't known, but it did herald the arrival of what, at that point, made the audiences who were familiar with the film feel as though they were hanging out with an old pal that hadn't changed much.

But as the stage lights came up to reveal a full-size boxing ring and two boxers punching the bejesus out of each other, anyone unfamiliar with the *Rocky* story was placed squarely into a seedy, dingy-gray milieu populated with steroid-pumped sweaty meatheads grunting out an opening number. Like it or not, this wasn't the Disney musical playing down the street a few blocks south.

Rocky prevails in the fight and earns 70 bucks but nets 41 after the payouts to the thug with the eyepatch. Soon we learn that our boxer also collects debts the "hard way" but won't break the poor hard-up sucker's thumbs if he "don't pay up." It's our first sign that maybe this Rocky guy is also a softie. By the time he sings to pet turtles accompanied by the mellow sounds of a nylon guitar, we're pretty sure we were right.

Looking out for him, Mickey, the crusty old boxing coach, advises Rocky to "[e]nroll in one of them trade schools" but Rocky assures the old-timer that he has plenty of fight left. Mickey has better things to do. But right now so does Rocky; his nightly appearances at the pet shop haven't gone unnoticed. Adrian, a shop worker, pretends she has no interest in him but once he leaves the store it's clear that he's been on her mind.

Rocky makes a stopover at Adrian's brother Paulie the butcher's meat locker (possibly—no, certainly, the only time in theatre history that a collection of hanging cattle carcasses elicited applause from an audience) to collect a debt for his thug pals. Rocky takes care of business and looks for Paulie, the sort of guy who claims that if he were Rocky he would've broken the guy's thumbs to get the money and then pulls a three-dollar bottle of whiskey from his apron and belts a shot. Paulie is certain that going to work for Gazzo the goon is a step up and asks Rocky to put in a good word. In return, Paulie asks Rocky to stop by the house on Thanksgiving. Adrian happens to be making the turkey.

Meanwhile, boxing champ Apollo Creed and his posse, including a trio of jazzed-up concubines, are in town to promote his January fight, but his scheduled opponent has broken his hand and withdraws. Thinking that billing the fight as Creed vs. "The Italian Stallion" will make a snazzy impression in the press and elsewhere, Creed and his handlers focus their efforts to acquire Rocky Balboa as Creed's stand-in challenger. Creed pledges to "carry him a few rounds then drop him."

Back in South Philly it's Thanksgiving night and Rocky's appearance makes Adrian uneasy. She is also galled at the fact that he was invited without her knowing. After some of the usual brand of domestic discord between Adrian and Paulie, Rocky convinces her to leave the house with him. Sometime later Adrian's chronic standoffishness begins to disappear. Rocky is dim but well-meaning and his dippy jokes and wisecracks prove an antidote for all the trouble at home, at least for this night. "Life is worth living with someone to fill in the gaps" he sings.

Later at Rocky's shabby apartment, Adrian reveals the reasons for her disquiet: She knows that Rocky is a "debt collector" and to boot she's never been alone with a man in his apartment, she tells Rocky. She also confesses "I don't like boxing." "I'd stop the world from spinning for you" sings Rocky.

Back at the gym, Mickey tells Rocky that Creed is looking for a sparring partner. Rocky readily accepts and Mickey doles out some tough love: "You become a leg breaker. You gotta have a little respect for yourself." He goes on to tell Rocky that he's wasting his life.

Under the false impression that he is in fact interviewing as a potential sparring partner for Creed, Rocky is taken aback when the fight promoter offers him 150,000 dollars, win or lose, to be the challenger. Rocky initially declines, but the promoter assures Rocky that this is his "big break" and that if he passes it up he'll be sorry for the rest of his life.

Street smart if nothing else, Rocky realizes that he is being played. "Here stands a fighter but they want a clown" and recognizing a precipice when he sees one, that he must go all in or not at all, nevertheless Rocky pledges to "make a new start" and to "fight from the heart."

Under a large banner that states the number of "days to the fight," some of the film's most memorable moments emerge onstage in Act II. Rocky drinks the raw eggs (spontaneous applause), Rocky runs up the stairs of the Philadelphia Museum of Art (spontaneous applause), and engages in training rigors that interlace with projections depicting Rocky in laser-focused isolation.

"Eye of the Tiger," the hit song from the film that has endured as an anthem representing the aspirations of anyone keeping their "eye on the prize," makes an inevitable appearance midway through Act II signaling, in case we have forgotten, that we are cascading on slippery ice toward a do–or–die denouement.

It's closing time Christmas Eve and Adrian tells the girls at the pet store that she is spending the evening with Rocky. A sloshed Paulie shows up and berates his sister, accusing her of having fallen too far into a hole under Rocky's spell. "You don't give a good Goddamned about your own brother anymore?" he barks at Adrian after prattling on about Rocky spending time in a wheelchair after fighting Creed. Paulie is shown to the door but later that night shows up at Rocky's apartment uninvited, claiming he is taking his sister "home where she belongs" but Adrian ushers him out. "I almost feel sorry for him," admits Rocky.

By now, Rocky is a hometown hero and South Philly is showing up for support at the boxing match, many with a "what's in this for me?" angle. Rocky is taunted time and again by doubt but gathers his resolve and pledges to "keep on standing."

Some theatre-savvy folks who saw and studied the show felt it their duty to opine that *Rocky* the musical had the same problem but at the opposite end that *The Lion King* the musical had. Each show had its own respective coup de theatre—*The Lion King* at the start of the performance and *Rocky* at the end, making the subsequent remainder of *The Lion King* all but unmatchable and the first two acts of *Rocky* to some degree diluted as one waited around for the grand finale. More arguable is that the uncanny alchemy of remarkable stagecraft coupled with full-bodied storytelling *was*, in fact, a "problem," but in the case of *Rocky*, it did lead many, including Ben Brantley, above, to point out that the brilliance of the finale served to illuminate the so-so conditions of the material that came before it. To most civilians, however, dramaturgy and craft aside, the sequence was what high-price ticket buyers coveted—a roller-coaster thrill ride that left the audience with a mouth and an eye full of candy.

"*Rocky* is a Broadway knockout," proclaimed Rex Reed in the *Huffington Post* review, calling the score "rich and serviceable" but going on to praise Andy Karl's performance effusively.

> He dances in and out of the ring with complex precision. He looks like a movie star. He's virile, he's in command of the stage, he's a one-man hormone explosion. He has charisma, a camera-ready physique from the cover

of *Today's Health*, and the kind of body language that leaves the audience transfixed from beginning to end. If *Rocky* ever ends, watch out for more big things from this guy. He is merely sensational.

Huffington Post *Review, May 13, 2014*

Reed went on to praise the boxing finale: "You have never experienced anything on a Broadway stage like the championship bout that brings the show to a screaming, tumultuous finale."

Most other mainstream critics were nearly unanimous both in their disappointment in the score and their admiration of the finale. *Entertainment Weekly* espoused that the songs in the show "merely shadowboxed with melody" and that too many songs in the show "played like missed opportunities." Yet, the 15-minute-long finale of the show received some of the best notices of recent seasons. Christopher Barraca's set was also widely acclaimed and he went on to deservedly win the Tony Award that year for Outstanding Scenic Design.

With all this buzz, there should have been, if history were to repeat itself, a sustainable lift at the box office. But there wasn't. So there was something counterintuitive happening here; even with a number of (semi-)rave reviews, supplemented with a number of (mostly) positive ones, even then dotted by a couple of stinkers, the box office takes didn't rise to the levels that one might expect. The percentage of capacity numbers hovered mostly in the low- to mid-70s (percent of capacity of 100), but by the time summer hit, this dropped into the 60s. And these, as any 44th Street bean counter will tell you, aren't sufficient to keep a big-budget musical afloat.

In addition to the subject of Broadway demographics as discussed earlier in this chapter, it should be noted that Broadway seemed to be running on a sort of "movies-to-stage adaptations" pile-on that season and in seasons just prior and was rather dulled by the prospect of more screen-to-stage enterprises. Notwithstanding the (literally) dozens of film adaptations for the Broadway stage in seasons prior that did or didn't find an audience, the likes of *Once, Newsies*, and *Kinky Boots* represented an acceptable standard of practice that musicals must rise to the occasion of. Conversely, *Doctor Zhivago, Ghost, Big Fish*, and *Bullets Over Broadway* were the kinds of adaptations that audiences and critics had little patience for.

In any final analysis, certainly it's better to be remembered favorably for one achievement than for nothing at all when a show closes. Sometimes this achievement involves revolutionary or particularly well-written subject matter, creative design and/or staging, a particularly riveting performance, or even some facet that was particularly well done but eclipsed by the shortcomings of the show itself. *Rocky* will likely fall on the side of the latter. The storyline of the musical ends in a happy place even if it doesn't end exactly as we had hoped with Rocky taking the world championship from Creed. But Balboa himself couldn't have been more pleased. After all, he doesn't get wheeled out of the ring in a wheelchair, he gets the girl and the money, and, oh, his nose ain't broke neither.

6

KING KONG

Opened November 8, 2018
Closed August 8, 2019

A one-trick pony can't carry the whole rodeo.

Key dramatis personae

Drew McOnie, Director and Choreographer: Olivier Award–winning director of *Strictly Ballroom* and others in London and beyond.

Jack Thorne, Script Writer: Award-winning English author of, among a host of other lauded work, the stage play *Harry Potter and the Cursed Child* for which he won the Tony and Olivier Awards.

Marius de Vries, Songwriter: Grammy Award–winning executive producer of the music for the *La La Land* film, among other notable film scores; wrote songs for *King Kong* and when other songwriters departed the project was the sole songwriter of the original songwriters still on board.

Eddie Perfect, Songwriter: Australian actor, singer, and songwriter; wrote songs for the New York iteration of *King Kong* and later for *Beetlejuice* the musical.

Sonny Tilders, Animatronics Artist: Designed and built animatronics for the *How to Train Your Dragon* tour, among others. Key designer of the *King Kong* puppetry.

Carmen Pavlovic, Producer: Director, CEO, and producer of Global Creatures. Lead producer of *King Kong* the Broadway musical.

Gerry Ryan, Entrepreneur and Producer: Founder of Global Creatures, an Australian production company that produced *King Kong*.

The adapters of this *King Kong* seem to have two stories they wanted to tell. One is a morality tale about the evil of trapping a living being in a cheap entertainment scheme. To judge from my own misery in the audience, I'd say this is a theme they mastered.

Jesse Green, New York Times, *November 8, 2018*

King Kong

Poor hairy guy. There you were, a lone army of one atop the Empire State Building, helplessly deflecting that barrage of bullets being lobbed at you with so little mercy and with such unabated cruelty. Yes, those New York critics sure can be tough on a guy.

In the same *New York Times* review as above, Green mentions that when reporting on a screen-to-stage adaptation he routinely questions the inherent value of the effort. What, if anything, was to be gained by the repurposing? Did the adaptation invite legitimate, original, modernistic points of view, for example? Or were the arteries of fresh perspective clogged by an adaptation that was a myopic mess despite emphatic assertions by well-meaning production types that it "really is deeper than it looks, folks, honest!"?

If you asked a seasoned theatregoer about the value of what rolled out on the stage of the Broadway Theatre in late 2018, most would report that it was all but dripping with pointlessness as a Broadway musical, 36.5 million dollars' worth of it, according to Securities and Exchange Commission filings. And this was despite what truly appeared to be noble efforts by the creatives to revitalize a storyline and infuse a modern relevance. But that fact was promptly dismissed by something more menacing than the silverback ape himself; the whole endeavor smacked of being mercenary, and that's not a pleasant word in theatre patois.

A common understanding of the word goes something like (my words, not Webster's): a greedy act or endeavor intent on (let's face it) raking in as much cash (in this case, presumably from the tourists) as one can. Now, as P.T. Barnum would tell you, this kind of razzle-dazzle opportunism is nothing new. But (and hold on to your bearded ladies and Siamese twins here) this time it was done with a 20-foot-tall, 2,000-pound anatomic gorilla with dopey, dewy eyes.

And for about the amount of time it takes to excuse oneself to the restroom and return to one's seat, it *was* a visceral thrill, one, in fact, unlike anything seen before on a Broadway stage. The problem after that? One had to endure the banality of a musical built around—and existing because of—a giant puppet, roundly parading itself as musical theatre.

But why not? Turned out the big fella boasts an impressive résumé on film, dating back to the genesis of the "talkies." Since then no less than eight major film releases have revolved around the ape. And so what if sequel titles like *King Kong Escapes, King Kong Lives,* and the no-nonsense *Kong: Skull Island* hadn't been runaway hits? The King was still the king and what was profitable for the goose of the film could as well be for the gander of the stage.

Walking With Dinosaurs had cleaned up at the box office as an arena show, earning upwards of a reported 455 million dollars in 10 years of touring. The show's website claimed that over nine million people had seen the show worldwide, and while that number loses some luster when compared with the estimated 70 million reported to have seen, for example, *Les Misérables*, the takeaway is that animatronics are, well, cool. They certainly are to the little nipper crowd who surely outnumbered the grown-ups.

Walking With Dinosaurs was an offshoot of a multipart BBC documentary that placed "live" dinos onstage through a clever pairing of automation and puppetry and framed the extinct creatures in their (staged) natural habitats. A good idea, really, given that there was an educational element.

Then from Global Creatures, the Australian-based producing organization, sprang the idea that a musical based on the *King Kong* films might not be the worst idea. But the show would have to smash technical hurdles and go where no musical had gone before. It was on.

Five years and six meters high of a giant ape later the show opened in Melbourne to mixed reviews. With no fewer than eight music and lyric writers, it's no wonder critics thought the show was choppy. As *The Age* reported,

> *King Kong* is a historic theatre event, a technologically sophisticated confection for the senses that you'll never forget … A somewhat flimsy book is the show's weakest link, and there are scenes where you feel your senses boggled as a substitute for, rather than a technique for enhancing, dramatic narrative.
>
> Playbill, *June 16, 2017*

But it takes more than lukewarm reviews to kill a show like this; the show extended the originally planned length of the engagement twice, likely due to the demand to witness the largest puppet ever to be created for the stage. With this kind of built-in interest, some future life might naturally be in the offing, but the Aussie critics were in consensus, claiming that the score wasn't particularly appealing and didn't do much to move the storyline along. Most also griped that the way the story was told in general was problematic. But the question remained as to whether this would all be taken into advisement if the show traveled east toward the brass ring of Broadway.

Spider-Man: Turn Off the Dark was closing. The show had needed to run for five years in order to gain back its capitalization and turn a profit but was packing up after only two and a half in Gotham. Since only a small clutch of theatres in New York were equipped to handle a musical on the scale of *King Kong*, it was a lucky break for the ape musical.

Original Australian director Daniel Kramer had departed the production and several directors, reportedly including John Rando (*Urinetown*), were approached, but eventually Eric Schaffer was named the director of record for the New York incarnation. Being obvious that the show required substantial overhaul of the script and score, the producers capitulated and went shopping, a reversal of the (astonishingly naïve) earlier plans not to make substantial overhauls and that, in the producer's words, "we're all happy with the shape that the show is in right now, and don't see a need to rush or make any major changes" (*New York Times* interview, June 26, 2013). Eventually that confidence was shaken, reportedly by creative team members and seasoned would-be investors who insisted that New York critics would savage the show if the storytelling wasn't clearer, the characterizations less generic, and the score less dull. Reportedly, Craig Lucas, the original scriptwriter, departed because of "creative differences," and much of the music used in the Melbourne production was thrown out too.

Marsha Norman and Jason Robert Brown had shelves of awards between them and when the brass at Global Creatures got an agreement from each of them to rework and tighten the screws of the *King Kong* script and score, jubilation was in the air. Between Norman's propensity for writing with a human psychology–enlightened pen and Brown's keen ability to write songs that frame characters from the inside out so artfully, the producers were confident that the pair would "humanize" what had become understood as a musical "spectacle" into a musical drama worthy of consumption by a serious audience not necessarily there for the visceral thrill of it all.

But the marriages ultimately ended in divorce after a two-year-long thorough exploratory period and nine drafts of the script. Although still finding the material compelling, Norman threw in the towel, explaining to the *New York Times*,

> I'm no longer involved with *King Kong* in a creative capacity, because *King Kong* has moved toward the nonstandard musical arena. We exhausted the possibilities, I believe, of what I could do in writing a book where the main character doesn't speak or sing.
>
> "*King Kong*'s Latest Victim: The Writer," Michael Paulson, October 16, 2016

Brown had been hired to simply augment the score, leaving much of Marius de Vries's original intact, but eventually Brown also found the show's proposed formatting an ill-fit, stating,

> I was only ever hired for *King Kong* on a per song basis—if there was a theatrical moment that they wanted a song for, they would ask me, and if I thought I knew how to do it, they paid me to write the song. Ultimately I wrote something like 12 songs, and then the creative team changed completely and decided that they wanted a different sound for the show, something more electric and "pop," which is not what I do. When I saw the finished show, it was abundantly clear that I would not have been the right person to write that show, and I'm very happy for them that they were able to fulfill their vision.
>
> *Interview with the author, December 11, 2018*

Following Norman's graceful exit the producers shut down the idea for a soon-to-be Broadway run, stating in a separate interview with the *Times*:

> We realize that there are some exciting creative changes we can and want to make before *King Kong* comes home to New York City and we don't want to be pressured to rush in to meet any artificial deadlines. We want to make the best possible show.
>
> *Carmen Pavlovic, producer; New York Times, March 6, 2014*

Now that the show had walked away, or been pushed forcibly by circumstance, if you prefer, from the Foxwoods Theatre (soon to be renamed again), another challenge was at hand since only a handful of the 40 Broadway theatres had the physical space to house the gargantuan requirements of the show. When one opened up because a show was closing, the producers must act quickly, and that fact meant that there was no time to dawdle.

Drew McOnie had helmed *Strictly Ballroom* in the West End, a show that Pavlovic had produced. When director Schaeffer and *King Kong* parted ways, McOnie accepted the directorial duties and assiduously went to work to ascertain how *King Kong* would unfurl as a musical for the stage—the solution to the puzzle that had addled and confounded so many.

Surely McOnie fast realized what Norman, Brown, and other transient creatives had some time ago: The effect of the puppet, while astounding to witness, was little more than a theatrical sugar high. If *King Kong* the musical was going to earn its mettle in the world's most discerning theatre environment, it must hoist itself up and hold its own through substantive writing and direction that must never serve as a "filler" or placeholder until the next time the puppet took the stage. These were the stakes; too many musicals had come and gone because of artistic death by deference of substance to form, truth to artifice, and material to stagecraft. Moreover, the audience must relate to and feel the same empathetic responses for a 20-foot-high inanimate controlled by 20 puppeteers in plain sight and others offstage working remote controls that it would for a human under the same duress.

The renovation began with many of de Vries's songs remaining and the score augmented by Aussie songwriter and performer Eddie Perfect with small print contributions by others. Hot ticket Jack Thorne had written *Harry Potter and the Cursed Child*, not an adaptation of a Harry Potter book but rather an original story told in two parts for the stage (one critic later suggested that Thorne's accepting the *King Kong* assignment must have been merely an act of "commerce"), and was basking in the afterglow.

Now "hearing" the show through the prism of the theatre-pop music sound and with the intention of the show unveiling itself as more than short-lived candy for the eye, McOnie and team realized what they believed to be the "vision." It wasn't that these same intentions hadn't existed in Australia, it's that they were a jumble in Australia.

The news broke in the spring of 2017 that the musical had found a home on Broadway and would debut in the fall of that year. However frantically the creatives were still rewriting the clock was ticking. Eddie Perfect was burning the candle at both ends. His musical adaptation of the *Beetlejuice* film was set for an out-of-town tryout at the National Theatre in Washington, DC, in the fall around the same time *King Kong* would set out on its way.

By late April the Broadway Theatre was sitting without a current tenant. The shuttered *Rocktopia*, which had taken up residence there in March, had closed its scheduled limited run. Principal casting for *King Kong* was announced and casting began to wrap-up by mid-June.

As the principal actors assembled in the rehearsal room, the puppetry team worked to navigate the broader to finer points of moving a mammoth puppet around a stage, a move that must eventually be executed with pinpoint accuracy. One cast member explained:

> The rehearsals were run almost in place of an out-of-town try-out. We rehearsed as two companies. One as the King's Company who learned the ins and outs of the movement capabilities of Kong from the Australian run, and perfected the moves to perform the moves and sequences seamlessly. The other half of the company consisting mostly of the leads and the covers rehearsed the scene work and music and choreography in an adjacent studio space. At the end of the day the King's Company would combine in the studio and catch up with the choreography and get plugged into scenes.

The advertising campaign announcing the show went into overdrive. Commuters from New Jersey, Long Island, and beyond arrived at Penn Station one morning to find the great landing hall inundated nearly entirely with massive posters depicting an ape on all fours in silhouette accompanied by the words "Alive on Broadway." The producers were smartly taking aim at the tourists and the bridge-and-tunnel demographic but didn't leave the deluge of ads there; they placed the image of the beast on taxi cab roofs, subway posters, and every other conspicuous locale. The message was clear: If you heard about the show in Australia and poo-pooed a Broadway iteration then check yourself—the Gorilla is on his way.

In the rehearsal room, McOnie was driving the point that the audience must be captivated by the storyline and without that interest the show would dwindle to a costly thrill-park ride. "Drew definitely wanted the heart and soul of the story to be just as powerful as the 2.5 ton gorilla," noted a cast member.

The press, however, seemed to care little of the morality tale emerging from the story being told and instead became infatuated with the technical elements of the show. Local and national press reported on the intricacies of getting this massive beast onto the stage and ran features marveling at the scope of the effort which was multiple layers deep to execute.

The small army that worked the ropes and the joy sticks that propelled the giant beast around the stage consisted of 10 onstage puppeteers while another three operated the motors and generated the Kong sounds from a booth in the rear of the balcony, a room nicknamed the "Voodoo Lounge."

In sum, according to the *New York Post*, the puppet ape held strong at 20-feet tall and weighed 2,000 pounds and inside it were 985 feet of electrical cable and 16 microprocessors. The industrial motors that controlled his facial expressions, which ran the gamut from puppy-dog wistful to grunts and roars for anger, were the same ones used in the Mars rovers by NASA.

As news spread in theatre circles that *King Kong* was actually going to materialize as a Broadway show, it seemed to generate equal parts curiosity and skeptical eye-rolling around town. One well-informed theatre insider recalled,

> I was in a staff meeting in mid-spring and someone mentioned that *King Kong* was on. I didn't believe it. I remember thinking, "Yeah sure." Then there started to be all this buzz. I thought someone would surely pull the plug or say "April fools" or something. It wasn't until I was walking down Broadway and passed the (Broadway) theatre when the posters went up (for the show) that it hit me that this was really going to happen. I went back to my office and called my husband who works at a hospital and told him. He didn't miss a beat and said, "Yeah, I saw it on a cab this morning. When can we go?"

If stirring up curiosity was the objective of the blunt, black-and-white posters with the ape silhouette, the strategy seemed to be working. Presale tickets were steady. The first eight previews were promising, boasting full houses. But at that point, the murmurs of skepticism turned full-throated. Word of mouth and Internet chatter were consistent: The ape is really cool but the show itself is a nonstarter.

It wasn't a stretch to agree with the armchair critics during the previews. The show seemed to be, as many had suspected it would, eclipsed by the stagecraft leaving many to gloat, "I told you so."

The opening moments of the show were encouraging. McOnie's choreography was athletic and urgent and the set vividly brought to mind a cold as steel, unforgiving era in New York when work was scarce and mouths were hungry. Ann Darrow certainly was. A spunky country girl, Darrow has come to New York to conquer her Broadway dreams.

In the audience, we didn't have to wait long for more clichés to appear. Our eager Ann, downtrodden from continuous rejection and the stars in her eyes now dimmed slightly, seeks refuge from the biting New York cold. In a diner she encounters Carl Denham, a bush-league movie director who offers her food. As Ann eats, Denham explains that he is shooting a movie and needs a leading lady, but the whole endeavor must remain hush-hush. Ann naively accepts, seizing the opportunity to save herself from the ravages of the streets and become a star, as Denham has promised.

Denham leads Ann to a waiting boat commanded by Captain Englehorn and with a large crew aboard. As the boat sails, the captain notices that another boat is following and, growing uncomfortable, asks Denham to explain. Denham deflects the question, later telling a suspicious Ann that the trailing boat is loaded with gas bombs that will only be used in case of emergency.

After a week at sea, tensions are running at a fever pitch onboard but Denham proclaims that they have arrived at Skull Island, quickly moving to take long camera shots from offshore. Once disembarked, the wary troop remains on guard as Denham films Ann climbing about the dense knotted vines.

Earthquake-sized booms are heard from the distance growing dauntingly closer. The star's entrance is more impressive than we had imagined. The seminal moment generates equal parts awe and lament; as one critic wrote, "[It] feels like a Universal Studios attraction setting up shop," going on to point out that "Times Square feels more like Orlando every day—except you can walk from each attraction and can still feed a family of four for less than $300" (Jerry Portfield, *Rolling Stone* magazine, November 9, 2018).

All told, history (and the critics) may well be the arbiters of the value of such an event, but for now the effect is (no other word applies) spellbinding.

The creature, its massive scope aside, appears strikingly "human" even from the start. The puppetry is executed and presented so masterfully that it is all but impossible not to buy in. Denham attempts to film the beast but Kong takes a swipe at him and smashes the camera. Ann is taken by the beast to a high cliff where she attempts to appeal to his good nature. Denham, terrified and angry, suggests that everyone should get off the island immediately and leave Ann behind, but then it occurs to him that if Kong could be captured and returned safely to New York all the world would clamor to see the great beast. And that would make him rich.

As a massive snake (puppet) threatens to lay fangs into Ann, Kong rises to her defense and is injured. Ann mends his wounds and the two forge a bond with one another. But as Kong sleeps, Ann attempts an escape. Halfway down the cliff, she encounters Denham and his sidekick Lumpy and Denham assures her that he has a plan to save her. At Denham's urging, Ann calls out to the beast to lure him. As Kong descends in pursuit of her, the crew is waiting with the gas bombs. Kong is captured.

It was the end of Act I but, like many musicals, especially the truly troubled ones that struggle in the second act, Act II is especially problematic for *King Kong* as a stage play. In this case, it wasn't that the storyline was fuzzy or the story telling skewed. The trouble here was that after Act I there was so little else to dramatize (save for the finale) to bring the show to a conclusion that what was put in its stead inevitably came off as tripe-ish pillow-stuffing.

Ann is anguished over the beast having gotten injured and in her participation in his capture. She expresses her crushing guilt to Denham but he threatens to ruin any chances of her ever landing a job in show business if she doesn't cooperate and participate in the show he is devising to reveal Kong to the public. Ann grudgingly agrees but feels as though she and Kong have developed a kindred bond and must see him. She assures the imprisoned beast that if both of them play their roles that all will turn out well in the end. Ann is shocked to observe that Kong has stopped eating and is effectively grieving himself toward a slow death.

It's opening night and Lumpy delivers flowers to Ann's dressing room, telling her that she's a good person and that good choices are hers to make. Taking this to heart, once onstage Ann refuses to call Kong onto the stage and reveal him to the world. Denham is furious and commands her to play her part and do as she has been told. She refuses, instead ordering Kong to fight back. She is pushed off stage but her screams from the wings awaken Kong and he manages to break free from his shackles and his imprisonment. Now loose and on the rampage on the streets of New York City, armies attempt to restrain the beast by whatever means possible.

Kong instructs Ann to climb onto his back and the two ascend the still-under-construction Empire State Building. Kong survives barrages of gunfire, destroying planes and taking bullets all the while. Finally, the hell-fire is too overwhelming and Kong succumbs, falling to his death.

Ann, heartbroken, naturally comes to Kong's defense, evangelizing that odd beings should not be subject to being put on display for greedy commercial purposes and that exploitation of that sort is indefensible.

The irony wasn't lost on many. You could smell it all the way down Broadway and Ann Street in lower Manhattan where Barnum himself first suckered the crowds into paying to see his own brand of shenanigans.

There again, you can't blame a guy for wanting to make a few bucks. And for a while the prospects looked promising. Preview and opening week audiences, driven by curiosity, nearly filled the Broadway Theatre with attendance numbers in the 90 percent and above levels. But once the reviews were released, those numbers quickly declined to the low-80s and 70s. By the middle of January, the numbers had declined further into the mid-60s. Given the universally awful reviews and word of mouth, it wasn't surprising that audiences were staying at bay. During those early days, one cast member was especially skeptical about the show's future, stating, "The truth is that we probably won't make back our investments because of our high operating costs." After all, there were 36 people onstage and another army behind the scenes.

The critic for the *New York Post* set the tone for what would consistently follow in headlining his review with "*King Kong* is a gorilla-size mess" and closing with "Early on, as the ship departs New York Harbor, the scenery, stagecraft and video projections merge so beautifully, you think this show may lead to someplace special. Nope. 'King Kong' is less fun than a barrel of monkeys." But by contrast, his review was the best of the heap, which ranged from sardonic ribbing to outright mean.

In a rare move, *New York Times* critics Jesse Green and Ben Brantley published a joint review, quipping as though they were the guests of honor at a Noël Coward bash:

> Green: Perhaps we are mistaken in applying arty standards to the cynical product of an ambitious entertainment company that made its name on animatronic arena shows. Character logic may not matter here as much as the intermission sales of the Kongopolitan (vodka, triple sec, cranberry juice, and a splash of lime). I looked in vain for the Kong-branded Thorazine.

Brantley: Gee, Jesse, it's enough to make you long for a margarita, with Jimmy
   Buffett melodies on the side.
Green: You are referring to *Escape to Margaritaville*, which until now was my
   musical theatre low point of 2018. Jimmy, I take it all back.

The orgy of stagecraft wasn't enough to keep *King Kong* open for even a year.
The attendance numbers went up and down but, surprisingly, did not reach the
kind of consistent lows that would suggest that a closing was looming or was a
foregone conclusion. On the contrary, the reported attendance numbers the week
before the show announced that it was closing were in the high 70s.

Regardless, the old boy hung up his fur and closed in late summer of 2019,
leaving many naysayers to mumble something under their breath about going back
to the theme park where he belonged.

7

ESCAPE TO MARGARITAVILLE

Opened March 15, 2018
Closed July 1, 2018

Silly is as silly does.

Key dramatis personae

Jimmy Buffett, Songwriter and Artist, whose persona and perspectives *sur la vie* guided the compass for the character realizations and overall milieu of *Escape to Margaritaville* the musical.

Mike O'Malley, Script Writer, Actor, and Writer: Known largely for his work in television, including the series *Shameless* (for Showtime).

Greg Garcia, Script Writer, Director, Actor, and Producer: Known largely for his work in television, including the sitcoms *Yes, Dear* and *My Name Is Earl*.

The Parrotheads, the millions of Jimmy Buffett fans worldwide. The most devoted have pet-named their children the Parakeets, subsets of the Parrotheads.

Christopher Ashley, Director: Tony Award–winning director (*Come From Away*) and artistic director of La Jolla Playhouse who shepherded *Escape to Margaritaville* from regional theatre to Broadway.

If ever there were a time to be drunk in the theatre, this is it.

Jesse Green, New York Times

Escape to Margaritaville

Peter Pan isn't the only one in show business who refuses to grow up. The other dissenter is Jimmy Buffett. And Buffett makes no apologies for that; his music has spun over 50 years of variations on what amounts to a few persistent themes: (1) avoid real work whenever possible and have a cold alcoholic beverage; (2) renewal, mental and otherwise, happens expeditiously in a tropical location, so come join in and have a cold alcoholic beverage, and (3) when necessary, give responsibility the middle finger and have a cold alcoholic beverage.

But to whittle Buffett's efforts into a near three-point package of irresponsibility and insubordination is far too shortsighted; the world of Jimmy Buffett also dwells in real grown-up trips like self-actualization upon reflection of age and character and assuming responsibility for what just might actually be your fault. And here lies the essence of the Buffett music and presumably his real-life persona, getting it all figured out while shirking too much adult responsibility while doing that. Escape to the islands and you'll get it all sorted out. Yes, that'll do the trick. You might even get yourself into a little bit of trouble while you're there, and hell, there's nothing wrong with that.

Given the worldwide recognition of Buffett as a "brand," if you're going to fashion a Jimmy Buffett musical, it's likely best to stick to these facts and don't stray that horse too far from the marina. The show did that. Nevertheless, the trouble with *Escape to Margaritaville* the musical is that so little horse *sense* went into the show's *raison d'etre* that it left audiences who attended the show and who weren't familiar with Buffett's oeuvre in a near-vegetative state.

The fact that *Escape to Margaritaville* the musical was largely pointlessness was in no way to castigate or underrate Buffett's entertaining music, or for that matter to lay blame at the feet of an exceptional production team who did the best they could with what possibly should have remained undone. But it does raise a relevant question worthy of a good think: In an era hell-bent on producing jukebox musicals, must so many artists with hit songs be exploited for Broadway fare, especially if the narrative storyline born from the union of song and conception amounts to two-and-a-half-hours of hooey? (Even *Mamma Mia*, that chestnut of jukebox shows, had a reasonably engaging storyline. *Smokey Joe's Café*, on the other hand, was smart enough to skip a serious attempt at a story and allowed the songs to stand on their own.)

It's no stretch to understand Buffett's appeal. The gist of the music being what it is makes you feel like cashing in and heading south, far south, with blatant disregard for the consequences of such a thing. Shirk answerability and duty. Chase younger women. Tell your boss to jump in a lake. But, of course, you can't do that. Jimmy has you covered, though, and with Jimmy you can at least dream about it a little.

Buffett has been singing about the freewheeling lifestyle since at least around the late 1960s, but the songs, often registering in a hybrid Country and Calypso vibe, seem to get fresher over time. His track record as an author is equally compelling with three best sellers to his credit. With all this to take into consideration, most of it overwhelmingly positive, creating a Jimmy Buffett musical must have looked a great deal like a no-brainer to the check writers.

"For 10 or 15 years, all kinds of different people have been trying to figure out how you wrap Jimmy Buffett into a new musical" (Director Christopher) Ashley recounts. "This is the first time Jimmy felt like people had created a show that honors the spirit of his music." By the time *San Diego Magazine* ran the story that *Escape to Margaritaville* the musical would premiere at the Ashley-helmed La Jolla Playhouse in California, the Parrotheads (the code name given to the most devoted of Buffett fans) already had the ice in the blender. The effort wasn't to be Buffett's first attempt at a musical. In the 1990s, a musical called *Don't Stop the Carnival* was scrapped after being savaged by critics. The show was a tale about a stressed-out New York press agent who ditches it all (not surprising) and moves to a Caribbean island to run a hotel (especially not surprising). Also predictable here was the inclusion of the usual array of Buffett themes including midlife crises and tourists covered in oil. Despite the blistering reviews, business was steady in Miami where the show opened. Said one cast member of the experience: "I didn't read the reviews. We were having too much fun. We even got extended. Jimmy and Herman (Wouk) worked on it (the show) again down in the islands (after the Miami run) but it just wasn't working." Buffett eventually walked away from the show, refusing (it was rumored) to replace Wouk at the behest of the producers.

La Jolla Playhouse premiered *Escape to Margaritaville* in 2017 with a script written by television and film writers Greg Garcia and Mike O'Malley (who has also written for the theatre) with direction by Ashley and, of course, songs by Buffett and his various writing cohorts. San Diego local reviewer James Hebert accepted the show as is:

> You will not be surprised to learn there's a good-time, party vibe to it all. No one expected this show to be *Les Miz* in flip-flops (much less Chekhov by the beach), but it's still worth noting how *Escape to Margaritaville* delivers just about every bit of what the phrase "Jimmy Buffett musical" promises, from the splashy colors to the steel-drum beats to the palm-fronded beach bar slinging fruity cocktails.
>
> San Diego Union-Tribune, *May 29, 2017*

Had other critics the following winter and spring viewed the musical through the same lens, the outcome might not have been the same. But the sharks were out and circling theatres down the road. "Landsharks," Buffett himself might call them.

The production team was encouraged by the reception in California, and La Jolla was no novice at developing and producing shows with an eye on Broadway. Those efforts can be largely rewarded; the regionals where a show is gestated typically take a piece of the action if the show is successful elsewhere (and eat the losses, if not), which is a sizable gamble. La Jolla, however, has turned out some of musical theatre's most popular titles from *Thoroughly Modern Millie* to *Jersey Boys* to *The Who's Tommy*, and if ever there was a house that was the blue chip among the lot, this one was it.

The show, now definitely pointed toward New York, would make a few stops along the way, a trajectory that resembled one that many large musicals would typically take en route; a steady line of theatres where it would continue to refine and polish ahead of the harsh New York critics and discerning New York audiences where, lest we forget, Broadway shows have no built-in subscription base that many theatres on the road do. Each Broadway show must sell single tickets, and that audience is hard-won. New Orleans, Houston, and Chicago were ahead. In the advance press Ashley told the *Chicago Tribune*,

> It is our hope that this show will make you feel like you have been invited to a party. We want to attract the Parrotheads, sure, but also the people who might know only one or two of Jimmy's songs.

The approach was savvy, the subtext being something along the lines of "don't expect *Death of a Salesman* at *Escape to Margaritaville*. Buffett was onboard with the philosophy that the show was to be only pure escapism. "I was not going to suddenly write something that did not pertain to a guitar player in a bar," he told the *Tribune*. Fairly warned, only later did the general show-going public realize how low the bar had, in fact, been set.

But Ashley's and Buffett's remarks also qualified for smart public relations; it wasn't necessary to be a Buffett fan to enjoy the show. "Keep an open mind," it subtly recommended. "Trust us, you'll have a great time." And even if would-be ticket buyers knew little to no Buffett music they might have encountered Buffett culture elsewhere in the form of merchandising. Buffett's hit "Margaritaville" has found its way onto the titles of everything from casinos to margarita mix to a popular restaurant chain bearing its name.

Of course those Buffett greatest hits found their way into the lot of *Escape to Margaritaville* as did other hits that Buffett claimed he had to play at his concerts or the audiences would revolt. The table was set and the strategy to pin down an audience was solid. After a few months' hiatus, the show left the safe, warm home field advantaged nest of La Jolla and opened in New Orleans, a safe harbor in itself in that it is Buffett's home turf, his music sometimes being monikered "Gulf and Western" for the signature that it places on that part of the United States.

Opening the short tour in New Orleans would seem like a good omen for Buffett. He had spent a great deal of time in the Saenger Theatre where *Escape to Margaritaville* would make its national debut; his uncle had sold 3D glasses out of this building in the 1950s and Buffett would often watch movies and shows from the balcony. Buffett reported that it was within that dwelling that he contemplated the life he had planned for himself as a shipyard worker but decided to change course and enter show business.

New Orleans audiences were enthusiastic, many loading up on a Hurricane (a tropical drink concoction indigenous to the Crescent City) and stumbling to the theatre from Bourbon to Rampart streets. That was about right for a party town crew. Other New Orleans theatregoers who were simply local theatre aficionados and not necessarily Parrotheads remembered the experience of attending the show more vividly than the show itself. Said one:

> The show outside the theatre was better than the show itself. Jimmy Buffett fans and New Orleans are a dangerous mix. There was a concert type … party atmosphere to it and people were raising hell and ordering drinks and getting sick in the lobby. It was like half of the audience was expecting a Jimmy Buffett concert and the other half was going to the theatre. It was bizarre.

Discounting those not throwing up in trash cans, some audience members reported that they were skeptical that the show would make it as Broadway fare where audiences, especially at hundreds of dollars a ticket, expect at least some modicum of substance. Said another first-nighter: "It (the show) was what it was but about halfway through the first act I realized that no great drama was about to unfold on that stage. Not tonight. But I expected that."

For the most part, it wasn't until the Chicago run that the show itself began to encounter serious criticism from the press, that open forum that has been known to save many shows from themselves with constructive feedback. But by that time too much structural revision was impractical and, moreover, the show had never promised to be any more than what it was. Many Houston critics had softballed any criticisms by and large, taking the show at face value:

> But hey, it's Jimmy Buffett. Just go with it. Enjoy the dancing zombie insurance salesmen, fully aware they are LSD flashbacks (!); wait long enough and those beach balls will arrive.
>
> *Chris Gray,* Houston Press, *November 2, 2017*

The *Houston Chronicle* review was equally as passive on the criticism:

> It's refreshing to see a show that doesn't try to be smart, edgy, political, emotional, clever, intellectual or even plot-driven. *Escape to Margaritaville* at the Hobby Center through Sunday, has none of those qualities. That's a compliment.
>
> *Wei-Huan Chen,* Houston Chronicle, *November 2, 2017*

But the temperature was colder in Chicago and so were the reviews. The capstone of the criticisms wasn't unpredictable. *Time Out Chicago* might have summed it up best:

> Plenty of those around me in the audience Wednesday night were delightedly humming along. For those of us looking for a story worth caring about,

though, the vibe here is just too chill. In the Buffett platonic ideal, these characters don't really have any problems—and dramatically, that's a problem.

Kris Vire, November 16, 2017

A crack in the "party-on and the show will be saved" philosophy of the show was beginning to form, widening each time expectations of more than a cartoonish degree of dramatic tension and depth of character were anticipated or expected. There were other words and phrases that were tossed about in the blogs and Broadway message boards to the tune of "if you're going to saddle us with drivel for the next two hours could you try to do so without insulting our intelligence?" Examples come to mind of previous jukebox shows that both didn't and did (remember *Good Vibrations?*) and by now there was, it seemed, an "it's too dumb to take it seriously" meter in the minds of more sophisticated theatregoers. With *Escape to Margaritaville*, the needle was jumping.

Most sang the same refrain: The storyline of *Escape to Margaritaville* played out with all the conflict, depth, and subtext of a child's Saturday morning sugary cereal box. The thru-line was a brew that could have (and did) echo themes of Buffett songs with plot-devised excuses to sing other Buffett songs shoehorned into it, but many thought it was too little too late. And for many, especially at moments like the one where the ensemble sings a (literal) ode to "Cheeseburger in Paradise" or dancing zombies appear onstage, yes, the show was intelligence insulting.

For what it's worth, the plot went something like this: Tully, the Buffett alter ego, is part-time bandleader and full-time horndog at a Caribbean beach resort. He regularly beds the female guests and then drops them like a coconut from the tree the moment their vacation ends. He explains his unique circumstance as a "License to Chill." Conversely, Tully's pal Brick is the "sensitive" tiki bartender.

Rachel and Tammy have "come down from Cincinnati" as resort guests and Rachel is the lucky winner of Tully's weekly conquest. Tammy is engaged to Chadd back home and Chadd has forced her to go on a strict pre-wedding diet, which incenses Rachel (read: no "Cheeseburgers" for Tammy).

And that's really the set up. Once the cliché characters are introduced, add some water and wait.

Tully and Brick take the girls' luggage to their rooms along with some margaritas (surprise), but Rachel is more concerned about her work turning potatoes into an energy source (you read that right) than in taking a vacation. Naturally, there is a volcano on the island (surprise) and Rachel wants to visit the volcano to take a soil sample. Brick offers to drive the girls up to the volcano and Tully tags along. Rachel explains to Tully that she has no time for any shenanigans in her life because her work consumes her, explaining that "It's My Job." Naturally Tully is now more determined than before to pursue his agenda and force Rachel to "chiiiillll."

J.D. is the local beach bum who regales guests with outlandish stories about his life. Certainly Marley, the hotel owner, thinks so. Soon J.D. is singing to the guests but not of seafaring misadventures or rescuing fair maidens. Instead he croons

"Why Don't We Get Drunk ... and Screw?" which the guests find great fun and a jubilant sing-along follows (you read that right).

If, by now, you yourself have fallen into said vegetative state, you may wish to flip ahead a couple of pages to the critical commentary.

No one would blame you.

Tully charms Rachel by teaching her to play a few guitar chords. Brick and Tammy are growing fond of each other and Tammy reveals to him that she is engaged, but not before they nearly lock lips.

Jimmy Buffett, uh, Tully, explains to Rachel that he had moved to the island to escape the cold, stress, and the "son of a bitches" of everyday life. Whether tropical magic or one too many "frozen concoctions," the two kiss. The next day Tully reveals that he believes he has fallen for Rachel.

Taking the high road, Brick attempts to dissuade Tammy from her urges to sleep with him and to remember her promises to Chadd, who had warned her previously of the male "sharks that can swim on the land" down in the islands. As a distraction, the two figure that getting tattoos (surprise) will do the trick. Tammy and Rachel discuss how they've changed during the past week before departing back to Cincinnati. Tully, Brick, and the company sing of "wastin' away in Margaritaville" as J.D. scuttles about looking for his lost shaker of salt (I am not joking), and Brick realizes all he has is "nothin' to show but this brand new tattoo" that bears an unmistakable resemblance to Tammy's face.

Tremors are felt. The volcano on the island is about to erupt. Margaritaville descends into bedlam.

But to us, as intermission settles in, rather than reflect on tattoos, missed opportunities at love, or the doom that an erupting volcano may bring, drinking sounds like the more attractive alternative. The bar is easier to find than a point. Turns out we are in luck.

Naturally, tropical drinks were on the drink lists at the theatres where *Escape to Margaritaville* played. The Broadway house in New York went full tilt as Jesse Green pointed out in the first paragraph of his review of the show.

> And the good news is that *Escape to Margaritaville,* the Jimmy Buffett jukebox musical that opened on Thursday, makes getting sloshed on Broadway easier than ever. The lobby at the Marquis Theatre has been kitted out as an island-style thatched-hut alcohol fueling station, complete with margaritas for $12 (on the rocks) or $16 (frozen), as well as bottle openers, koozies, and other drink-oriented paraphernalia.
>
> The bad news is that you still have to see the show.
>
> *Jesse Green,* New York Times, *March 15, 2018*

Cheers, Mr. Green, we'll get through this together.

If you returned after intermission you found everyone onstage running for cover. An escape boat is readied but once all are aboard J.D. is discovered to be missing. Brick and Tully find J.D. in the jungle, digging frantically for a buried treasure. With the escape boat having now left the island, the group makes tracks to J.D.'s plane. Despite his pilot's license having been revoked (don't ask), he will fly them off the island to safety.

The "treasure" that J.D. had been unearthing was family mementoes from an earlier time. Turns out that J.D. hasn't always been the village beach bum but has actually (surprise!) lived a sordid life, some of it tragic. Having lost his wife (and child), J.D. insists that Tully tell Rachel about his feelings for her and offers to fly him to Cincinnati.

At her rehearsal dinner, Tammy discovers that Chadd has set her up with vegetarian fare to be in line with her diet. Brick, Tully, J.D., and Marley, the owner of Margaritaville, crash the wedding dinner and Brick insists that Tammy forget the vegetarian fare and instead have a (yep) "Cheeseburger in Paradise" during which the cast sings and dances the eleven o'clock big production number, in this case a rousing ode to the, um, cheeseburger. Tammy comes to her senses and punches Chadd and Tully confesses his feelings to Rachel but she tells him their relationship wouldn't last. His depression is short-lived, however, once he is approached by Ted, a music agent who tells Tully he'll make him a star.

And the rest you've already guessed. Everyone, including J.D. and Marley, eventually end up happily together. Margaritaville is rebuilt and Tully becomes a singing star.

The play may be over but the hangover sets in. For *Escape to Margaritaville*, it came in the form of the critical response and the resulting box office take, which hadn't been particularly swell to begin with.

The reviews ranged from caustic to conditionally so-so. John Simon remarked that there was not "one original thought" in the whole of the musical. Other critics agreed:

> How could Buffett and company, in this fun-starved beach party, so deleteriously have taken their eye off the ball? Oh, speaking of, at the end of the show, hundreds of beach balls are dumped on the audience. One of them ricocheted off the top of my head. It was the only thing all afternoon in the Marquis Theatre that I didn't see coming.
>
> *Peter Marks,* Washington Post, *March 15, 2018*

Marks went on to call the show "insufferably dumb."

The *New York Post* led with the headline "*Margaritaville* musical is a paradise for Parrotheads—and no one else." Audience members echoed the viewpoint. Said one: "I thought the music was okay but I only knew a couple of the songs. So I didn't understand a lot of the jokes either."

Some critics were more positive, accepting the show for what it was: "This jukebox musical is the theatrical equivalent of sipping on a frozen drink while lying on a beach chair in the blazing sun. It's not good for you, but it feels good," said Frank Scheck in the *Hollywood Reporter* review. Scheck and many other critics also praised Ashley's "clever" staging and the choreography of Kelly Devine. The work of script writers Greg Garcia and Mike O'Malley wasn't reviewed as favorably, with critics using words like "weird," "weak," and reeking of "sitcom" to describe the outcome. But with lines like "I was addicted to the hokey-pokey, but I turned myself around" well, really, what would you expect the reaction to be?

But the reviews, in this case, were in reality only of trivial consequence. *Escape to Margaritaville* would have been tough to sell at high ticket prices on any long-term basis. The Buffett fans would have turned out, sure, and the crowd just looking for a certain gratuitous escapism. But the box office statistics indicated that enough of either wasn't enough to pay the bills and keep the show open. The Broadway League documented that the show started strong in previews (most or many do) with the percentage of filled seats dropping into the 60 percentile within a few weeks, later declining into the 50s, and finally ending with a death spiral of high 40s and low 50s, numbers that cannot sustain large musicals, in most cases.

But for Parrotheads across America who missed the show before it closed up shop in New York, there was welcome news. A non-equity (a production in which actors and stage managers do not receive union protections or benefits) tour was launched in the fall of 2019. Week-long engagements, longer in larger cities and shorter in smaller ones, were a much more viable business plan for the show.

In "Margaritaville" the song, the singer contemplates if a "woman's to blame." In the musical that later appropriated its name from the song, it was the damn fault of narrow thinking that was the downfall of the show.

8

GLORY DAYS

Opened May 6, 2008
Closed May 6, 2008

Great, even good, theatre takes time.
Slow down.

Key dramatis personae

Eric Schaeffer, Director: Visionary co-founder and Artistic Director of the
Signature Theatre in Arlington, Virginia; well known for rethinking large
musicals for smaller stages and championing young writers' work.

John O'Boyle and Ricky Stevens, Lead Producers: Guided *Glory Days* to
the Broadway stage only a few months after the show's initial run at the
Signature Theatre.

Nick Blaemire, Music and Lyrics, Actor, and Songwriter: Made his Broadway
debut as an actor (in *Cry-Baby*) concurrently with his Broadway debut as a
Composer and Lyricist for *Glory Days*.

James Gardiner, Book Writer: Made his Broadway debut as script writer for
Glory Days.

But if this show is an almost complete failure, it's not a travesty you can take
perverse pleasure in watching implode. That it's so full of promise and so
empty of everything else isn't just the breaks—it's heartbreaking. This is not
just because authors Nick Blaemire (music and lyrics) and James Gardiner
(book) are, respectively, 23 and 24 years old, but because none of this ever
had to happen.

Matthew Murray, Talkin' Broadway *Review, May 6, 2008*

Glory Days

It's best not to try to make sense of some things. Charlie Chaplin once came in seventh in a Charlie Chaplin look-alike contest. Pizza boxes are square but pizzas are round. Stephen Sondheim didn't win the 1984 Best Score Tony Award for *Sunday in the Park with George*. And the premature transfer to Broadway of the little engine musical *Glory Days* is another confoundment.

In an opening night interview, the show's director, Eric D. Schaeffer, gushed over how pleased he was with the show and called it a "breath of fresh air." Others poured out superlatives over the cast and the writing team. What none revealed outright, however, although it was reported that many knew, was that opening night and closing night for the show would be one and the same. This would forever attach a "B" for "bomb musical" on its chest, an infelicitous label that perhaps it could have been spared if producers hadn't been in such a hurry, even taking into account business sense and a few lucky breaks.

Other musicals have suffered the same destiny of opening and closing contemporaneously. Whereas even distinguished flops like *Carrie* and *Merrily We Roll Along* managed to squeak out a few performances before the ax was dropped, some others died hasty deaths within hours of the opening night curtain coming down. Some standout examples come to mind of the (as of this writing) 22 Broadway musicals that have opened and closed concurrently: *Dance a Little Closer*, a show graced with the sure-footed writing of Charles Strouse and Alan Jay Lerner, opened and closed the same night in May of 1983. Looking back further, Yul Brynner, known for having brought the King to blazing life in *The King and I* on Broadway, tour, and film, suffered the embarrassment of playing only one regular performance on Broadway in *Home Sweet Homer*, a show with music composed by Mitch Leigh, the composer of *Man of La Mancha*. This was in spite of the show having had the advantage of playing a year on the road, more than enough time to fix the show's ills. And there was *Kelly* in 1965 that had the talented Mark "Moose" Charlap who had composed most of the music for *Peter Pan* aboard.

But of all the shows that were orphaned on opening night, few, if any, had (as *Glory Days* was) been ripped from the womb of development and hurled onto a Broadway stage as mere musical caterpillars. Theatre, musical or not, takes a village to get it right, and the villagers often come in the form of audiences and contributors of and to several incarnations of the show before it lands in Gotham or other major theatre hubs as "all grown up."

Come From Away, the Broadway musical, played four regional theatre tryouts before creators and producers brought the show to Broadway, allowing ample time for then chipping away of any extraneous or unfocused elements. *Million Dollar Quartet*, another Schaeffer-helmed musical, was another in the line of Broadway musicals that stopped at regional theatres along the way for the necessary tending and pruning. The list, especially in recent years, is populated with some of musical theatre's most revered titles.

But naturally not all shows have the good fortune of regional theatres taking them under wing as they mature, though, and most will, as discussed at length in this volume, find a way through other means. Remember *Spider-Man: Turn Off the Dark*? Michael Cohl, the lead producer, resorted to passing out audience questionnaires in order to get formative feedback on the audience responses to the show, unable to travel the show out of town before Broadway. Still others will roll the dice and play one out-of-towner attempting to gather as much wisdom as possible before a Broadway opening. This route is sometimes deceiving and hardly bulletproof; Sting's musical *The Last Ship* tried out in Chicago and had audiences enthusiastic and critics optimistic, but the show barely registered with audiences in New York, closing after a few months.

The night *Glory Days* premiered at the Signature Theatre in Washington, DC, Peter Marks, the local theatre critic for the *Washington Post*, was in a cheery mood. Marks, known for a particularly acerbic tongue when irritated with a show or some element therein, turned in a particularly upbeat review to the copy desk that winter day.

> The buoyant product of the talented young team of composer-lyricist Nick Blaemire and librettist James Gardiner swiftly, tunefully and yes, authentically latches onto the rhythms of late adolescence and plays them back to us as the music of wrenching transitions.
>
> Washington Post, *January 25, 2008*

However, Marks' review was not absent constructive feedback; to this end his reporting was both objective and fruitful, particularly about the show's pacing and character development. Naturally, the feedback and positive responses had the *Glory Days* team celebrating with victory laps up and down the streets of Arlington. But there was more to celebrate in a derivative theatre cosmos where movies-to-stage adaptations are the new normal, *Glory Days* was an original story reportedly based on Blaemire's own experiences.

As for the newcomer writers Nick Blaemire and James Gardiner themselves, any ulcers that had developed as they released their little bird from the nest abated after Marks chronicled his encouragement. Those ulcers would return and worsen within a few weeks.

Eric Schaeffer's track record as co-founder and artistic director at the Signature Theatre is impressive: He is largely responsible for the theatre's recognition and honor with the 2009 Tony Award for Excellence in Musical Theatre, a hard-won accolade that places on the institution a mantel of greatness won by a mere few top tier of regional theatres. The Signature has also won scores of regional awards for excellence. Schaeffer is widely applauded for his revisioning and mounting of both large-scale musicals as smaller entities, thereby dispensing with much of the spectacle ballyhoo and digging deeper into the heart of the story. He is also well known as a champion of new musical theatre writers, encouraging their development and on occasion mounting their work.

Schaeffer soon realized the potential in the budding writers' idea for *Glory Days*, offering them a production, a boon for any theatre writer but a windfall for unproduced fledglings. Whatever the outcome of *Glory Days* and whatever role Schaeffer may have played in the wisdom of bringing the show to New York with such haste, it must (at least) be offset by his offering a platform for young writers. Naturally Blaemire and Gardiner accepted. At the time of the production, the writing pair were both in their early- to mid-20s.

It had happened many times before. In the last couple of generations alone, Stephen Schwartz was in his early-20s when *Godspell* and *Pippin* arrived on New York stages and made him the talk of New York. Stephen Sondheim was 27 when Tony and Maria made their vows in the original *West Side Story*. Jason Robert Brown had a show on Broadway as composer and lyricist before turning 30.

But, as discussed previously, the difference of theatre development of old and new is that, due to high production costs, assurances of name recognition by producers, and an array of other bank account draining expenses (skyrocketing legal fees and advertising costs among them), precious few opportunities exist for new work to be seen and heard, particularly by way of a production at a choice regional theatre where all eyes are wide open.

As the hubbub settled down in Washington, commotion was ramping up just over 200 miles away in New York City. To the background of buzzing phones, dinging texts, and flurries of emails, a couple of lead producers were eyeballing the Washington reviews with considerable interest. There had been a movement of late that suggested that Broadway musicals need not involve spectacle to sell tickets and *Glory Days* had the right alchemy. The popularity of *In the Heights*, *Passing Strange*, *Xanadu*, and others was creating a groundswell of sentiment that the era of the large cast, sensory overload show was in retreat (remember *The Pirate Queen?*) and smaller musicals were falling into favor. This placed primacy on the story itself doing the heavy lifting and absolved production teams from creating shows in which the technical elements and the staging must be done to the tune of "bigger is better," a charge that could take years to implement. This was to say nothing of the time required to raise the money to pay for the abundance of razzle-dazzle.

The *Glory Days* overhead costs must have leapt off the financial proposal like no other show had in recent memory. Given the number of people to pay the calculus was, certainly in relation to larger musicals, highly attractive. Four onstage actors and two understudies backstage. One set. A four-piece orchestra. A coming-of-age story that tugged at heartstrings and an attractive score that brought musical vibe of *Rent* to mind. Of course, all the excitement was bolstered by the encouraging out-of-town reviews. But somewhere in that flurry of office emails and those turbocharged text messages, perhaps no one in New York was fully considering the implications of what the reviews were *also* saying.

Any clouds of doubt elsewhere were parted by a spate of good fortune for the producers. At the precise moment that the first incarnation of *Glory Days* was receiving encouraging notices, another small musical was closing up shop and vacating the intimate Circle in the Square Theatre leaving it tenantless. *The 25th*

Annual Putnam County Spelling Bee had camped out in the space for over a thousand performances, playing to solid audience numbers since 2005.

Producers know that early birds get worms and a 776-seat theatre like Circle in the Square meant that an intimate show like *Glory Days* would find an appropriate home. It may have been a spontaneous move that involved buyer's remorse later, but this kind of serendipity didn't happen every day on Broadway. The producers secured the theatre and managed in somewhat short order to gather the funds to bring the show to New York. The show was now steaming toward a late spring opening.

There was more low-hanging fruit. An April preview period and early May opening would dodge a number of potential bugaboos that happen on Broadway with regularity. First, the show would begin performances still riding the wave of the Washington buzz. By way of example as to how critical this can be, *Honeymoon in Vegas*, a dandy of a show that transferred to Broadway from Paper Mill Playhouse where it got strong notices, is thought to have lost much of its momentum in the extended time lapse between its regional debut and coming to Broadway. Moreover, the show would open with enough time to make the cutoff for Tony Award eligibility. If a show doesn't open by that hard deadline at the official end of the Broadway season then it must wait until the following year to be considered for nominations, and producers are loathe to keep a show open over a year with no Tony Award wins or nominations to boast about in advertising. Finally, a sooner than later opening would keep the cast and production team intact and hence not run the risk of losing them to the employ of other shows.

But there was a downside and it was a humdinger. Two months is hardly enough time, especially in fifth gear, to properly take the show back to the typewriter and workshop rooms to implement changes, the precise kinds of revisions that critics of the show in Washington had stated were needed. To further complicate the possibility of a proper revisionary period to occur, Nick Blaemire was making his Broadway debut that spring as an actor in a new musical called *Cry-Baby*.

Nevertheless, from a producer's business perspective, the move made sense. From a show perspective, it was a dice roll at best and tantamount to theatre suicide at worst.

The *Playbill* online cover photo was captivating: The four guys who made up the *Glory Days* cast in an aerial pose after a full-hearted jump from the bleachers, behind them a wall of lights. No Madison Avenue superstar could have crafted this leadoff campaign better; the photo brought to mind a show that must have taken its cues as a kind of *Wonder Years* vehicle for the stage. Moreover, it captured a sentiment that these sparkle-toothed coming-of-agers were staring down a bright future and grounded in the playful atmosphere of a time when banter about superheroes and teenage sexual conquests were the most favored subjects in matters conversational.

As less than a week of rehearsals commenced in New York before technical rehearsals began in the theatre, concern was growing that tickets weren't moving. The low-key advertising campaign hadn't helped and it was suspected that the producer's modus operandi was to generate as much word of mouth as possible to get the word out. Privately, the executives were fretting.

"Papering the house" is a term that refers to complimentary tickets being given away to fill the theatre seats, the theory being that those recipients will tell their friends to see the show and steady ticket sales will follow. During previews, the papering of the house for *Glory Days* was rampant. In week one, although 43 percent of the seating capacity of the theatre was filled, the show only monetarily fulfilled 10 percent of its potential, a worrisome number at best. Still, the businessmen genuflected to the gods of ticket sales and prayed for a steady uptick once word got out that this was a show worth plopping a hundred bucks down for.

But as one exited up the stairs at the Circle in the Square postperformance the overheard rumblings betrayed that hope. Above all, the audiences seemed confused, not about the subject matter necessarily but more about why this show at this stage would take up residence in a Broadway house. One audience member pointed out that the effort would have been far more appropriately played if it had been in an off-Broadway or experimental space, a "safe" space as theatre people like to call it, where the show about growing up could have done a little growing up too.

Broadway isn't safe and the critical climate tends toward harsh and unforgiving. The average audience member left *Glory Days* wondering what was in it for them. The 90-minute show seemed directed toward a demographic that by and large didn't have much in common with them, save for a few plot points.

Will, Andy, Skip, and Jack were all best friends in high school but went their own ways after graduation. Will and Andy have remained in each other's company as college roommates, but Skip and Jack had departed to other colleges. On this night, a year after high school graduation, Will invites the other three to join him at a late-night meeting on the football field bleachers for a reunion. But Will has ulterior motives: As a prank, the four will set the sprinkler system off on the field during a reunion football game to get even with the jocks who ostracized them during high school. The boys brag about their college sexual exploits and rib one another incessantly. Finally, Will reveals the true nature of the meeting and the others agree to go along with the prank after some resistance.

Jack reveals that he is gay and Andy feels ill at ease over this. Nevertheless, Will convinces Andy to stay with the group. Skip reveals that he has had a catharsis of his own about the generation that he and the other three have grown up in. "There's a new world order," he sings; "Generation Apathy."

The four discuss their own postgraduation revelations and it soon becomes evident that the reunion didn't turn out as hoped. Jack searches for his friends' responses to his announcement and further reveals that he has feelings for Will. The two are surprised by Andy and Skip and an altercation ensues. The four become increasingly at odds with one another and one by one take their exits. Will is left alone onstage to contemplate "My Next Story."

The week two grosses were dismal. Positive word of mouth was traveling in reverse, with eight previews only totaling an aggregate attendance of 22 percent.

Four-fifths of the theatre seats were gathering dust as the producers read the box office reports while clutching Pepto-Bismol.

The decline in attendance and hope felt less precipitous and more like a slow-motion plane crash, as only it can on Broadway. Finally, after 16 previews, the show opened to expectedly poor reviews. Critics were less unkind speaking of the young, green, writing team, choosing instead to censure the guys in the suits. Some, like Mathew Murray in his review, above, went so far as to nearly defend neophyte writers. Critic David Rooney wagged his finger thus: "The producers have done an extreme disservice to the inexperienced creative team by shoving them into the spotlight with what's likely to be a commercial embarrassment" (*Variety*, May 6, 2008).

Washington critic Peter Marks, whose initial encouragement had resulted in mixed blessings for the show, opened his Broadway review thus: "Somebody was in an awful hurry to get *Glory Days* to Broadway, and in the end, hyper-acceleration may not have been the optimal speed for the move up I-95."

Marks did not backpedal nor did he have reason. For anyone who fingered him as the catalyst of the Broadway run, he set the record straight:

> The show deserved a lot of encouragement. But as I also tried to point out in a supportive initial review, it also needed some further elucidation, especially in the transitions between songs, in the fleshing out of the relationship among the four young friends.

As to his overall impressions of the Broadway version, he spilled in print what many already knew and were openly discussing:

> It's unfortunate that an interim development phase has been skipped, because as an entrant in Broadway's intense seasonal bake-off, the *Glory Days* that opened last night at Circle in the Square feels a bit undercooked … From what can be gleaned in a second visit, *Glory Days* has not been tweaked with any discernible impact since its Northern Virginia debut.

John O'Boyle and Ricky Stevens issued a statement the morning after the (mostly) blistering reviews: "We adore 'Glory Days' and everyone connected with this production. Sadly, given the overnight reviews and our low advance sales, we believe it is prudent to close the show on Broadway immediately."

A few days before opening, Nick Blaemire, in an interview, said, "As much as I welcome anyone's opinion, I have to stick to my guns. I'll survive. Because at the end of the day, it's just a musical."

9

BULLETS OVER BROADWAY

Opened April 10, 2014
Closed August 24, 2014

Past performance does not guarantee future results.

Key dramatis personae

Susan Stroman, Director and Choreographer: Broadway's wunderkind with a
trunk of Tony Awards in tow.

Woody Allen, Book Writer and Author of the screenplay: Controversial
American writer/director/playwright/actor and film director with an
astonishing variety of output.

Glen Kelly, Music Adapter, Arranger, and Lyric Adaptor for *Bullets Over
Broadway*; Stroman's redoubtable right-hand man.

A Bevy of Composers and Lyrists of songs that deservedly are included in what
is known as the *Great American Songbook*.

The cardinal sin in adapting a Woody Allen film comedy for the stage is
forcing the funny. So the creators of *Bullets Over Broadway* the musical, the
sledgehammering act of period-driven-desperation that opened Thursday
night at the St. James Theatre, have a whole lot to answer for.

Peter Marks, Washington Post, *April 10, 2014*

Bullets Over Broadway

Crimes and Misdemeanors, the Broadway musical? A morality tale of a mature oph-
thalmologist who enlists his hooligan brother to arrange a hitman in order to knock

off his lonely, middle-aged flight attendant girlfriend when she makes threats to squeal to his wife? You'd probably lose the family audience.

Annie Hall, the Broadway musical? An existential tale of a plucky girl and a neurotic guy who obsessively mulls over where the relationship went amiss and over the futility of existence? Eh. The New Yorkers might buy it but tourists want production numbers.

Bullets Over Broadway, the Broadway musical? For the 1994 film writer and director Woody Allen (who also penned the above) had (with co-writer Douglas McGrath) cooked up a riotous tale that dwelled where Allen himself is most at home when comedy is on his mind: broad, dark, and poking at stereotypes. Sweetening the pie was the ethos of an era and the Jazz Age music of that era that Allen himself is so enamored of. Did this have the makings of a musical? Then there were gangsters and gun molls. There were showgirls. There were showgirls who cozied up to gangsters and all make for zany musical comedy fare; remember those comic-relief mob types in *Kiss Me, Kate*? Or the dizzy showgirls from *Crazy for You* and *The Producers*? How about themes of Broadway dreams and making it in lights (remember *42nd Street*)? Those were there too. And one can't ignore those countless other shows where a nobody gets in bed with the devil and realizes that giving the devil his due might not have been a swell idea. All were onboard in *Bullets Over Broadway*, so no surprises here, but yes, there was certainly fodder for a terrifically entertaining, if formulaic, musical.

But then again, there's little sin in the formulaic if an originality in approach accompanies it. Susan Stroman is a director and choreographer who is so impossibly inventive and resourceful that there are few who come close; who else can take a spool of theatrical thread and spin it out with such inventive aplomb that it forces an audience to consider what devil she must have sold *herself* out to? If you find yourself in want of hard evidence here, you'll want to remember earlier Stroman shows; there's more than enough to make a slam dunk case out of it for any jury of theatre peers and civilians alike. In short, she is a marvel.

Stroman first put a stake into her own patch of Broadway real estate in earnest with *Crazy for You* in 1992. The choreography was the real star of the show eclipsing in impression even the golden Gershwin songs at hand. Her resourcefulness was perhaps most notable. Gold mining pans, vintage telephones, and chorus girls transforming into stand-up bass instruments were all provisions for Stroman's uncanny abilities to take simple props at hand and a savvy imagination and utilize them freshly and with a sense of humor.

Yet there was another far-reaching element of consequence to the arrival of *Crazy for You* in 1991 as Frank Rich summed up in his *New York Times* review:

> When future historians try to find the exact moment at which Broadway finally rose up to grab the musical back from the British, they just may conclude that the revolution began last night. The shot was fired at the Shubert Theatre where a riotously entertaining show called *Crazy for You* uncorked the American musical's classic blend of music, laughter, dancing, sentiment,

and showmanship with a freshness and confidence rarely seen during the
Cats decade.

With *Crazy for You* as a backdrop, it was evident that shows that were lodged in a
certain musical theatre antiquity still had legs. The "musical comedy" brand, having
been all but out of favor to British imports at least since the early 1980s, was still,
so it seemed, a hot ticket, certainly with the good graces of Stroman in the room.

If you need a musical theatre history lesson here, the "musical comedy" brand
mentioned above may be described thus: During the early part of the 20th century and as late as the 1940s (and even beyond), American musical comedy was
more entertainment and "escapist"-based than the trends of shows that followed as
musical theatre evolved as vehicles that were more intentioned to provide any social
and/or moral awareness. The plotlines were relatively simple and uniform: There
was a girl and a boy and some factor, which was situational, preventing happily
ever after from ever-aftering. During the 1920s when young girls were chopping
their hair off and slipping into flapper outfits, both of which represented liberation,
sometimes this emancipation was the subject matter, as the fairer sex faced choices
involving independence over adherence to "old" conforms.

The musical scores of these shows were often written by the popular composers
of those days (many had cut their teeth in "Tin Pan Alley") and the songs themselves were often so generic that a song could be plucked from one musical and
easily parachuted into another musical with little adaptation, and often at nearly the
same point in the plotline. And often there was a bevy of hardly covered chorus
girls, plenty of onstage misunderstandings, and, especially during the prohibition
era, gun molls and mobsters at a time in American history when, for whatever the
reason, mobsters were revered and glamorized.

So, viewing a show like *Bullets Over Broadway* in the context of all this looked
on the surface like the comfortable fit of an old shoe. But for *Bullets Over Broadway*,
there was a curious fit and untying the knot as to the reasons for that is much more
complex that the razor-thin storylines of those musical comedies.

To those who may not have followed his career (or aren't old enough to
remember), Woody Allen appears engrained in the collective awareness as the
overtly neurotic New Yorker filmmaker who spoons out hefty doses of existential dialog and characters who appear perpetually dissatisfied with the state of their
relationships. Of course, this fare is often couched well within a comedic premise
and with a male character (in the image of Allen himself, it is most often presumed)
in the male protagonist role.

But whatever existentialisms Allen has introduced and spun out, and for all the
dark as night dramas he has written and (sometimes) starred in, Allen was always at
his essence a natural theatrical comedic writer. In the 1950s, Allen began to write
for television and stand-up comedians which led to a number of books of short
essay comedy. He hit a stride in the early 1960s as a stand-up comedian himself and
by the middle of the decade he was writing and directing his own films. As a natural
monologist, the spirit of the theatre was never lost on his writing and this naturally

carried over as a fit on the Broadway stage. His early plays were hits. *Don't Drink the Water* played nearly 600 performances on Broadway and *Play It Again, Sam* clocked in at 453. Both featured actors who would later become bona fide stars because of their work in his films. By the late 1970s, it would have been all but impossible to stop the average person on the street in New York and other metropolitan cities, ask if they had ever heard the name Woody Allen, and be met with a "no I haven't."

Allen's work as a playwright had but a modest amount to do with his fame as it was the films *Annie Hall* and *Manhattan* that were game-changers for him. In the latter, the recurring theme of "older man desires/dates/struggles with feelings for younger woman" first came to the fore as a key dramatic device for Allen, and one that would become ubiquitous. Allen would often center a film around a leading man (sometimes with the telling tics of Allen himself in the mix) who would experience the same "taboo" love affair conflicts that appear to have obsessed Allen himself. Although there was never a clear line in the sand as to where Allen left off and the onscreen persona began, the pervasive nature of the conflict was often evident to anyone who paid attention.

Art imitates life. And the other way around, but for Allen in 1994, during the writing and production of *Bullets Over Broadway*, the film, it hit hard. In an announcement that shocked many but surprised fewer, Dylan Farrow, Mia Farrow's (with whom Allen had had a multiyear relationship) adopted daughter, alleged that she had been sexually abused by Allen for years. There was of course public outrage, denials, more accusations, litigation, and general word-against-word, but eventually state attorneys elected not to charge Allen.

One suspects that the film version of *Bullets Over Broadway* represented a much-needed respite for the cataclysms that Allen could not shake when off the movie set. For filmgoers it was a welcome romp. And for others, certainly given Broadway's affection for exploring any and all film material that was a reasonable prospect for turning into a stage musical, it looked like manna from heaven. As early as 2010, *Playbill* online followed up on a *New York Daily News* story that a stage version was in the offing and Marvin Hamlisch's name was mentioned as the would-be composer of the show. Hamlisch, for all the success that *A Chorus Line* and his film scores had brought him, hadn't had a true hit show in years, the last being *They're Playing Our Song* in the late 1970s. As successful as his early hits were, Hamlisch had had an unfortunate proportion of Broadway disappointment too; his *Smile*, *The Goodbye Girl*, and *Sweet Smell of Success* were all met with audience apathy and none ran long, although critics applauded the composer's efforts among other particulars. Were *Bullets Over Broadway* to come to the Rialto with a Hamlisch-penned score, then that could perhaps be viewed as a major draw for potential investors and for an audience demographic, particularly theatre party groups, that were old enough to remember his earlier hits and his marvelous film scores.

But Woody Allen wasn't especially compelled by what Hamlisch was bringing to the table and, being notoriously secretive about it when a project is in development and production, reportedly wasn't pleased that Hamlisch had granted confirmation to the press that Hamlisch was involved. Eventually Hamlisch and lyric writer Craig

Carnelia became unassociated with the project and for a while the line on *Bullets Over Broadway* the musical went dead.

But then Letty Aronson, Allen's producing partner (and sister), suggested that perhaps another option was to fashion already composed musical selections from the era for *Bullets Over Broadway*. At this point Allen, with a zealous affection for the music of that era (to the extent that it's nearly impossible to find an Allen film without it), became game once again. Glen Kelly was hired to adapt, arrange, and music direct the new musical that now featured a score by various composers, all long dead. The move was well within Allen's comfort zone, allowed him a near autonomous level of control over the music for the play, and meant that Allen was not required to collaborate at the extensive level that a book writer and a composer must during a musical creative process. It was an ideal setup for Allen. It was also where the trouble began, according to some critics. As we know by now, jukebox musicals were a staple of musical theatre. Broadly defined, a jukebox musical can be monikered such if the music contained therein was not originally written specifically for the show for which it is now being utilized. It need not be by the same music writers and, in fact, often it isn't. *Bullets Over Broadway* optioned for both circumstances whereas other jukebox shows optioned music by the same songwriter(s) to be utilized.

Allen, a clarinet-playing Dixieland jazzer of renown himself, likely knows every song by every songwriter written before the 1950s Rock and Roll invasion and champions that music at every opportunity. The music selected for *Bullets Over Broadway*, obscure as some of it was, did a masterful job of framing the underbelly of New York in the Jazz Age in an atmosphere of rough and tumble machine gun toting "crew" men and mob capos, the kind you don't want to get on the wrong side of. There was also low comedy and innuendo that stopped short of being rattling and unlined the essence of the characters admirably. Cast members on the production praised the songs chosen for the score. Veteran Broadway hoofer Synthia Link remembers: "It was really special to be a part of a show that took place in the '20s with authentic '20s music. It just made it feel good for us." Another cast member noted the same: "The songs made the show work in a way that an original score wouldn't have."

"Up a Lazy River" made clever appearances each time Cheech the hitman disposes of a body into the Gowanus canal. "The Hot Dog Song," rife with obvious innuendo, becomes a showstopper for Olive as she attempts to convince David and Julian of her versatility, and much lesser known gems like "The Tiger Rag" became showstoppers as Stroman spread the wealth. One number, a tap ballet for the gangsters that brought to mind a tap-dancing rendition of "Crapshooters' Ballet" from *Guys and Dolls*, brought down the house. When a lyric didn't quite fit, Glen Kelly and pen stepped in to revise (smartly).

The plot for the musical was uncomplicated and mirrored the film. Young playwright David is anxious to have his latest play, *God of Our Fathers*, produced. Moreover, he wants to direct it, feeling that the success of his first two plays was thwarted by directors who didn't understand or appreciate the depth of the material.

David and his idealistic cohorts believe that art should be for art's sake and not "sold out" commercially to appeal to the masses and make money, which is what David has none of and therefore can't produce the play himself. Try as he might, David's usual producer, Julian Marx, can't locate anyone to invest money in having the play produced because of David's inexperience as a director and his unyielding demand to direct the play himself, so the project is at a frustrating and disheartening standstill.

Nick Valenti is a larger-than-life New York mobster with a bubble-headed girl-friend named Olive. Olive is a club entertainer who longs to be revered as a true actress and to play a lead in a Broadway show, although any modicum of talent is conspicuously absent and she has the disposition of a petulant child. Willing to do anything for her, Nick agrees to put money up to produce *God of Our Fathers* and allow David to direct but only under quid pro quo; Olive must play the leading role. At this point, David will consider any reasonable proposal, but this one is out of the question and he offers Olive a secondary role, which she initially balks at but is ultimately convinced to accept. David and Julian pray that the other actors in the production will be strong enough to provide a reasonable distraction from Olive's incompetence on the legit stage.

Paranoid that Olive may stray or anyone else may require some reminder about who was making all of this possible, Nick assigns one of his goons named Cheech to keep an eye on her and, if need be, throw some muscle around in the form of broken kneecaps or worse. David finds that directing a Broadway play, even his own, isn't as simple as it looks, especially when grappling with the temperamental antics of leading lady Helen Sinclair who is desperate for a hit show, not having had one in years.

Sinclair feels that her role as written isn't an appropriate fit for her glamorous persona ("The character is so ... colorless," she complains. "I usually play more overtly heroic women. Even when I played the Virgin Mary I refused to play her as a virgin") and begins to badger David into rewriting the part to suit her. Rumor has it that Warner Purcell, the only male in the cast, has a binge eating problem, especially in times of strife, although all things appear to be currently under control (they aren't in reality).

Fellow actress Eden Brent can't be separated for long from her pet Chihuahua and the dog's constant presence irks Helen Sinclair endlessly. There appears to be more backstage drama than onstage drama when Olive begins dalliances with Warner when Cheech the goon is looking the other way.

But it turns out that Cheech isn't the knucklehead in the room that the theatre folks take him for; he is in reality a highly intuitive dramaturge, impressive with his (unsolicited) insights into what is "wrong" with the play. David, however, is unimpressed and mockingly dismissive after Cheech attempts to clear up the confusion of a particular scene. Everyone else, however, takes the Cheech guidance under advisement, urging David to accept his advice and revise the play. David quits in light of what he perceives as the passengers steering the ship.

Once David cools off, he finds himself more and more often in the company of Helen, who remains hell-bent on having her way with the direction her character, and therefore the play, are headed. David reveals to her that he is finding himself falling in love with her.

As *God of Our Fathers* heads out of town to begin the pre-Broadway tryout, David is by now fully enthralled and entrapped with and in Helen's charms. When David's girlfriend Ellen shows up at the train station because David has forgotten his lucky sweater, David all but dismisses her. Her suspicions that David has another love interest elsewhere become founded when later she discovers the sweater left behind on the ground. David has already left for Boston without giving it (or her) a second thought.

"There's a New Day Comin'!" sings the cast as Cheech's suggestions seem to have turned a dry, didactic play into a juicy hit. "The work you did on the play is great. And so *different* for you," says Ellen. Henchman-turned-playwright Cheech instructs Warner to stay away from Olive, in line with the edict issued by Valenti, conceding to David that Olive is terrible in the play. As such, Cheech has all but written her out of the play. "I don't want her in my show!" commands Cheech. "Whadda ya mean *your* show?" answers a disgruntled but realistic David, hanging on by a frayed thread to what he himself has written but no fool that Cheech's contributions have essentially guaranteed a hit in New York.

David is growing more and more enamored by Helen every minute and she appears to return his affections, telling David that he must choose between Ellen and her. "I Ain't Gonna Play No Second Fiddle," she harangues.

Having had enough of Olive's antics and under the cover of darkness, Cheech sends her "Up a Lazy River" reasoning that Olive's understudy can take over the role. Cheech, now feeling proprietary over the changes for the better that he has wrought for the play, begins to throw his weight around via the barrel of a gun.

Meanwhile David confesses to Ellen that he is smitten with Olive. Ellen retorts that she has "Found a New Baby" of her own, but there is little time to dwell; the news comes that Olive has been knocked off and David instantly knows who the killer must be. David confronts Cheech about the murder on the opening night of the show where Olive's understudy is being readied to go on. "You saw her acting," Cheech says. "It was a mercy killing!"

Goodfella Valenti suspects Cheech did his girlfriend in and plans to avenge the killing. Backstage at the theatre gangsters and actors are "Runnin' Wild" and Cheech is pierced with a bullet.

Opening night is a smash. Ellen returns to David at the opening night party. Cheech, now "Up a Lazy River" himself, is unable to claim credit for the play himself.

Valenti, now satisfied that mob justice has been served and is cognizant that he will make money off the play, rouses the crowd with a "that's life" number ("Yes, We Have No Bananas").

Curtain.

So why did *Bullets Over Broadway*, a hymn to a bygone glamorous American age and replete with the gold-plated acumen that it had, close on Broadway after only four months? A precise answer is a tall order but it is comparisons, of all things, that might have been the killer.

The Producers, as discussed in this volume, had inspired a tectonic shift for the Broadway musical. Lauded by many as the "funniest Broadway musical ever," the show is now the stuff of folklore, which might go something like "If you didn't see it with the original stars you can't possibly imagine how hysterical and clever it truly was." While much of the show's success was in direct relation to the performances of original stars Nathan Lane and Matthew Broderick (this was confirmed as business fell off when the two actors left the production), it was Stroman who had steered the whole endeavor, and brilliantly so. Whether the hype over the show was hyperbolic or not depends on who you ask, but no question remains that indelible visions of the show remain in theatregoers' memory banks.

The comparisons, if they existed in audience members' minds, were, unhappily for *Bullets Over Broadway*, echoed in the *New York Times* review, laying a counter argument that critics' pens haven't the same power as they once did over the staying power of a show, and, one suspects, may have been the comparison piece that to some extent spelled doom for *Bullets Over Broadway*.

In days gone by, if a powerful critic panned a show, particularly the *New York Times*, it was all but doomed to fail. These days that power seems to have abated, but nevertheless critical responses still hold a great deal of sway. But those who blame Ben Brantley, the *Times* critic, for attacking the show because it wasn't *The Producers* are missing the point. Brantley took issue with *Bullets Over Broadway* not because of what it *wasn't* but rather because of what he argued was an awkward (if not ill-) fit between director and material. Many others, like Peter Marks in his review above, found the show guilty of audaciously "forcing the funny."

Stroman "likes it big," espoused Brantley, loudly suggesting that she is at her best when shepherding broad humor, as in Mel Brooks humor, which (his words) is "Billboard Sized." Allen, by contrast, is "more likely to mutter," asserting that "[t]his makes her a natural ally for Mr. Brooks and a dangerous one for Mr. Allen."

But while Mr. Brantley and other critics felt that Allen's humor was done a disservice by Stroman's broad approach, other critics were less philosophical and embraced the show for the romp that it was intended to be for the stage and even if it wasn't, well, *The Producers*.

Elysa Gardner of *USA Today* mentions *The Producers* within the first few paragraphs of her review and then only to suggest that *Bullets Over Broadway* may turn out to be Stroman's biggest hit since. But then Gardner lets any other comparisons go soon enough, preferring to dwell upon the state of things present rather than drawing comparisons to the past. The welcome result was an all-out rave review for *Bullets Over Broadway*, adorning the show with three and a half out of a four-star rating.

Other critics agreed with Brantley and had other complaints, said Chris Jones of the *Chicago Tribune*:

> But when you translate Allen and Douglas McGrath's' backstage comedy to the Main Stem, somehow the *Great American Songbook* starts to feel a bit

like a cop–out … With a fresh, funny, zesty score, "Bullets" would have been unstoppable.

"The Producers," a show that is an obvious comparison, had such a score. In some ways, Stroman treats Allen's humor as if it were Mel Brooks humor. The two great comic writers are not, of course, the same. Brooks always goes for broke with a gag. Allen typically retreats, for a beat or two, into the cerebral. That is not as easy a style to translate to a musical.

Whether or not the criticisms in the reviews left the box office for *Bullets Over Broadway* too reverently quiet we cannot know. They certainly didn't help. But no awards don't do a musical any favors either. *Bullets* opened in early April and did receive six Tony Award nominations that year, including one for Stroman for Best Choreography and Allen for Best Book. A Best Musical nomination was strikingly absent. The box office take had remained steady, if not abundant, and this suggests that despite the couple of blistering reviews the show received, the favorable ones had won the day. A few Tony Awards would give the show a boost and so the bean counters sat tight.

Tony Awards presentation night came and went without a single win. The box office began to wane. As the calendar turned from May to June, prime awards season on Broadway, then so did the fortunes for *Bullets Over Broadway*. The first week of June saw a precipitous fall with attendance dropping into the 60 percent range. Following the Tony Awards shutout, the attendance numbers began to drop further, and with the show playing to half houses staying open became untenable.

Regardless of the unfortunate fate of *Bullets Over Broadway*, the show demonstrated that Woody Allen is a writing voice that should be most welcome on Broadway.

Maybe *Annie Hall* the musical isn't such a terrible idea after all.

Postscript: Three and a half years after *Bullets Over Broadway* made its Broadway bow, more controversy arose for Woody Allen and, by extension, the show. As the United States began a national, overdue dialog centering around sexual harassment and specifically sexual harassment in the workplace, Allen came under fire over remarks made to the press citing a "witch-hunt atmosphere" and warning against a culture in which "every guy in an office who winks at a woman is suddenly having to call a lawyer to defend himself."

In light of the remarks and the tension in the air, Goodspeed Musicals, one of America's most venerable theatres, cancelled a planned production of *Bullets Over Broadway* stating that

> In light of the current dialogue on sexual harassment and conduct, the author of *Bullets Over Broadway*, Woody Allen, has come under increasing scrutiny. Ongoing reports in the media have made this situation even more difficult and complicated, and this led us to reconsider the appropriateness of producing the show.

A high-profile production of the show might well have given the show a new lift post the Broadway disappointment and opened doors to a healthy regional theatre life. Instead, the bad publicity and scrapped production at Goodspeed appeared to drive another nail into the show's coffin.

10

DANCE OF THE VAMPIRES

Opened December 9, 2002
Closed January 25, 2003

Too many chefs make for unsavory soup.

Key dramatis personae

Jim Steinman, Composer: Rock and pop music songwriting and record-producing giant.

Michael Kunze, Librettist: Authored several German and international musical successes and translated and readied many English-language musicals for the German stage.

Michael Crawford, star of *Dance of the Vampires*: Having formerly starred in the title role in Andrew Lloyd Webber's *Phantom of the Opera* on Broadway, Crawford was also an international recording and concert star with many Broadway and West End outings of note.

John Rando, Director: Helmer of *Urinetown* on Broadway (for which he won the Tony Award for Best Director) among other significant credits in New York and elsewhere.

John Caraffa, Choreographer: Former Twyla Tharp dancer and celebrated dance and movement maker for *Urinetown* and the 2002 Broadway revival of *Into the Woods*.

It's not an outright comedy ... but as a serious musical—well, it's pretty damn funny.

Charles Isherwood, Variety

Dance of the Vampires

Remember Cousin Nettie? She's that wise, sassy old owl in Rodgers and Hammerstein's *Carousel* who didn't only crack about "doubtin' Thomases" and Virginia creepers huggin' bejeepers. She also had some pretty sensible advice about livin', keerin', and pokin' yer nose in other people's business.

Nettie surely would have had a mouthful to say about *Dance of the Vampires*, the Broadway incarnation that opened at the Minskoff Theatre in early December 2002. She might've crooned things like "don't produce a show that really is two separate shows at odds with one another" or "don't hire a leading man, even one with a winning track record, who turns out to be more trouble than he's worth" or even "don't believe everything you hear—especially in show business." But we'll get to all that, and believe you me, it's one hell of a tale.

Let it be known straightaway that the creatives of the show were no slouches. In fact, very much the reverse. One critic summed up the point most succinctly in his review when speaking of the creative staff and cast: "This is a production that inspires you to check your program open-mouthed at intermission to make sure you didn't misread it."

But despite the colossal misfires and general ill-judgment, the real hell of it all was that the show was a sizable hit in Europe, and if the creatives had stuck to that version then perhaps this tale of musical theatre woe on Broadway wouldn't need to be told. But they didn't and it does if for no other reason than as a cautionary one that goes something like this: "don't sell yourself out."

Yes, there was a time way back when that everything with the show was pretty swell and hunky-dory, but that version, which opened in Vienna in 1997, was called *Tanz der Vampire*. The show made sense even if it wasn't a masterpiece, but by the time the show hit Broadway … well … for now let's just take note that the show called *Tanz der Vampire* and the show called *Dance of the Vampires* were, in fact, two very different shows, written by the same person … er, people, well sort of.

Roman Polanski is nothing if not a filmmaker of consequence. His life story, however, will break your heart. Upon hearing the name, most people of a certain age will remember that Polanski was once married to actress Sharon Tate, who was pregnant with their child when she was brutally murdered by members of the Charles Manson gang of crazies. Polanski, many fewer know or remember, was also a Holocaust survivor, his mother having been murdered at Auschwitz. His father survived the unthinkable brutality of the Mauthausen camp, and Polanski himself eventually escaped the Krakow ghetto, wandering the countryside alone, or so the story has been told.

The indelible images of all he had witnessed as a young child, naturally penetrated his creative mind and many have shown up most strikingly in his films from the macabre *Rosemary's Baby* to the poignant *The Pianist*, the Academy Award–winning film about a Polish musician escaping German persecution during the unthinkable days of the Holocaust.

Roman Polanski and *Dance of the Vampires* intersected in a most dramatic and unusual way. In 1967 a film by Polanski entitled *The Fearless Vampire Killers* was released in the United States. In the United Kingdom, the same film was titled *Dance of the Vampires*. The film, essentially a send-up of horror movies, understandably wasn't to everyone's taste but Polaski received nods. And that was that.

Ten years and a couple of cinematic masterpieces later, Polanski was arrested in the United States and charged with drugging and forcing sex on a female minor. A plea deal was reached that involved Polanski pleading guilty to a lesser charge but Polanski, upon learning that the judge hearing the case was likely to give him prison time, saddled up and left, all the way back to Europe. Now a fugitive from justice, if Polanski attempted to reenter the United States he would be remanded to police custody. He has remained abroad since the 1977 exit.

Got it? Now, put all that in your pocket and we'll move on.

As we know by now, musical theatre fare beefed up in size and themes throughout the 1990s, much of it in and from Europe. Well noted, of course, are the West End transfers to Broadway that at that time all but obliterated the "small" musical (there were exceptions) in favor of spectacle and grandiosity, and German-speaking audiences had preferences that tended toward the same. Michael Kunze, a German, was the preferred facilitator of English musicals translated and adapted into the German language and sensibility. In the late 1980s and throughout the 1990s, Kunze was the point person for those traveling over German-speaking borders, adapting, among others, a great number of shows in the formidable Andrew Lloyd Webber canon and claiming a number of significant libretto writing credits of his own.

Kunze at one time claimed to have a certain proprietary right to having to some extent developed or at least be a principal practitioner of something called the "dramamusical." He explained the concept this way:

> The dramamusical is a tool to make clear that this is not a typical Broadway-type musical, which is more a musical-comedy. In what I do, we do drama with music. The way I write the shows is that I basically write the drama, of course with the music in mind, but the music is something that comes next, like a movie. The music is a very important element, but the most important element of the drama is the story, so the music really serves the story, and the music doesn't really have a right in its own beside the story, like a number that is just made for the music and the dance.
>
> Interview with *Broadway World*, November 7, 2009

Kunze appears to be suggesting that American Musicals are primarily Musical Comedies that did not evolve into vessels that place dramatic action at the fore and which the other elements principally serve, namely the music. To make such a claim of course smells of being underinformed at best and outright arrogant at worst, but the benefit of the doubt will be granted. More troubling is that Kunze seems to suggest that, as he defines it, the alchemy of the "dramamusical" is "new" and, moreover, not of American descent. And them's fightin' words, sir. It doesn't take an army of musical theatre aficionados and practitioners to inject any number of names and titles to refute his assertion.

At a minimum, Mr. Kunze's remarks clarify the intentions of the brand of theatre he espouses and the prevailing modus operandi of *Tanz der Vampire*, German style.

The story goes that the guy to credit (or blame, take your pick) with bringing the Polanski film to the stage was Rudolf (Rudi) Klausnitzer, a theatre impresario, manager/director, and owner, along with Polanski himself. Kunze was an obvious choice to helm the libretto.

If Jim Steinman wasn't the first name that came to mind when considering a score writer for the show, then why not? While his credits included a respectable amount of writing for the theatre (he had penned the lyrics to Andrew Lloyd Webber's music for *Whistle Down the Wind* most notably) his track record as a wildly bombastic, progressive songwriter preceded him. Rocker Meat Loaf may have been the winningest beneficiary; *Bat Out of Hell* and two sequels (written as a trilogy) with songs written by Steinman had sealed both Meat Loaf and Steinman's place in Rock and Roll history in the mid- to late-1970s by becoming one of the best-selling albums of all time. The album's cover art alone was as recognizable as songs like "You Took the Words Right Out of My Mouth" and "Two Out of Three Ain't Bad" that appeared on the album, but it might have been the unusual and unique structure of "Paradise by the Dashboard Light" that was most intriguing, nay, *theatrical* in form. It was extended, it was radical, and it was a status symbol of "cool" if you owned it.

Steinman was hardly a single album/concept hit wonder. He later supplied hefty hits for Air Supply, Bonnie Tyler, and Celine Dion and has a hit song catalogue that was known to be selectively, even in fragmental format, repurposed and placed into his musical theatre writing engendering an instant recognizability. Presto.

With *Tanz der Vampire*, steered by Polanski at the director's wheel and Steinman and Kunze as the primary writers, Austrian and German audiences got what they craved in the Wagnerian operatic sense, which, to wit, was through-composed, other-worldly, and possessed a certain mythical grandeur. With this in mind, to comprehend the true reality of the scope of the changes made to the production for the Broadway outing, one must recognize the specificities of the style that appeared in the German production, which one might classify in an era obsessed with labeling something like "grand pop-opera."

But when you give 'em what they want, you may be richly rewarded. *Tanz der Vampire* surely was. The stagecraft alone, that is to say the physical production, was likely enough to bring those who might find that the story was exasperating into the theatre to have a look. Big-budget sets and effects were aplenty and abundant enough to rival the visuals of the great European opera houses. Side by side with other operatic conventions like quintets that brought to mind those of the great opera makers of the 19th century and lovers whose togetherness was imperiled by other-worldly shenanigans, the show was a brazen example of the intertwining of musical theatre and operatic sensibilities—vampire style.

Never argue with success. Repeat it. Vienna, Berlin, Stuttgart, Hamburg, and other European cities all took a bite with productions of the show, many with multiple-year runs.

With all of the European success, naturally plans were put into place for a transfer to New York. But then, like a warning shot fired from over the bow of the boat by the gods of theatre, there was immediate trouble. American legal authorities refused to allow Polanski to set foot on American ground without being taken into custody for skipping the country years earlier. Arguments were made and proposals proposed but, even if as a matter of principle after all these years, Polanski had no cards to play. The New York opening was pushed out again.

According to some familiar with how things unfolded from there, Steinman saw the Polanski exclusion not as a setback but as an opportunity, giving Steinman himself more creative control. Steinman, it's been said, went to Kunze and pointed out the traps that the current European version of the script (there had been some revisions since opening in Vienna) would fall into in American translation. Neither Kunze nor the German team had reason to doubt; Steinman appeared to know American theatre and theatre custom well having been writing it for ages and particularly having spent several years under the wise tutelage of Joseph Papp at the Public Theatre.

But prospective producers and investors didn't feel safe by a long shot when it was floated that Jim Steinman himself might direct the show if Polanski wasn't ultimately permitted into the United States. The idea was later scrapped but not before Steinman, in efforts to assuage naysayers publicly, claimed that he had directed much of the European version of the show, often doing so without Polanski's knowledge or blessing. Whether or not true we'll have to take Steinman at his word, leaving us ultimately to draw the conclusion that with colleagues like this one better keep their guard up.

As discussed here, in 2001, *The Producers* stemmed a significant break with the recent past on Broadway. Elephantine musicals, many of which were crossovers from Europe, had held sway over Broadway ticket buyers for some years, with storylines grounded in overcoming mighty adversities of the far greater variety than boy-gets-girl-loses-girl and then through wits and wiles gets-girl-back of the musical theatre.

The Phantom of the Opera, Les Misérables, and *Miss Saigon,* among the most undeniable examples, were big-throated and abundant in every sense and had led the charge for many a would-be theatre writer to "go big or don't bother." The imitation efforts of the latter rarely paid off, but the musical writing gestures of the day are well documented. With a nod to playwrights Kaufman and Hart, many thought that the current state of the Broadway theatre, that "fabulous invalid" that appeared to be in critical condition careening toward irrelevance (but that had always bounced back until now), wouldn't make it this time. Others feared that the theatre of wit was an endangered species and the very traits of theatricality that playwrights like Kaufman and Hart had perfected were in woeful decline.

The Producers, the Mel Brooks stage adaptation of his cult-followed late 1960s film, gave oxygen to an old convention: high, witty musical comedy that was spiked with bawdy, sardonic humor, stereotypes ribbed in good fun, and a bouncy and unpretentious score. The timing was spot-on for this combination and the show won every conceivable award and accolade that year. But the show seemed to represent more than the revival on musical comedy; there was the feeling in the air that a U-turn of sorts was occurring and that more than an anomaly perhaps the show was actually a signpost and that commercial theatre ground was perhaps looking backward toward the future. Or so the market research showed.

All of this made some *Dance of the Vampires* producers and creatives bristle. As conceived, the show was entirely antithetical to what appeared to be the new trend in New York. The intention to bring the show to Broadway had been around since the conception of *Tanz der Vampire* but with changing landscapes the timing might be off, or so thought the brass. There was of course also the known taboo—an elephant in the room that couldn't be ignored. Musicals centering around other-worldly events and beings just didn't arouse much interest for New York audiences. Up the street at the Metropolitan Opera, not surprisingly, conditions were far more ripe for such things which naturally coursed through operatic veins. Operagoers in fact rarely gave such unorthodox subject matter a second thought. Broadway, how-ever, tends to snicker.

Still hopeful, producers and creatives thought that if *Dance of the Vampires* could ride the coattails of its mega musical cohorts, maybe it would capture an audience share rather than bear witness to the death knell of the mammoth musical.

David Sonenberg, Steinman's manager and at this point de facto lead producer of the Broadway version of *Dance of the Vampires*, rallied successfully that in accordance with prevailing statistics, the show must be transformed to meet new American tastes and expectations to achieve success with American audiences. This meant, in essence, that the new version should dispense with much of the European *sturm und drang* and more resemble the spoof-y climate of the film. "We were told to put five jokes on every page," Steinman later reported.

Steinman had been developing and writing a musical version of *Batman* with playwright David Ives, who was a well-known playwright and adaptor of theatre works and other literary sources. Ives agreed to come onboard as the key point person to give the "new" version of the show a facelift that reflected a much lighter tone.

As this strand of the *Dance of the Vampires* story was playing out, finally, according to press reports, a producing team stepped forward with interest. Anita Waxman and Elizabeth Williams had together produced the recent hit revival of *The Music Man* and it was reported that they initially had two requests: that Steinman step away as director and that a book writer be selected who met their approval. They had John Caird in mind to do both. Steinman protested, loathe to relinquish his title of dir-ector. After quibbles and squabbles, the compromise was that Caird and Steinman would co-direct and that Caird would also contribute to the book.

A reading of the script was held in New York in the spring of 2001 to assess the progress thus far. Steve Barton, who had originated the role of Krolock in *Tanz der Vampire* in Europe and was praised widely for it, read the role in New York, having reportedly had a verbal agreement that when and if the show came to New York he would come with it and reprise his European role. Who that verbal agreement was allegedly with isn't clear, but Barton felt confident that his award-winning outing would be repeated for New York audiences.

But within a few months Barton would be found dead.

It was reported from someone on the inside of the production that Waxman and Williams soon began to balk as production talks went along in earnest; although there was a list of potential investors that included some of the German producing team, it seemed that no one, save Waxman and Williams, had actually put any significant dollars into the coffer. The two decided to hold and see who else would pony up before making any more radical moves.

As this was happening, the script and score were being carved here and pruned there. Using the so-called trend research as their guide, the writing team was creating an entity that was, according to Steinman, part Mel Brooks and part Anne Rice, adding adjectives that one doesn't see paired together often, like "Wagnerian" and "funny." Regardless, the balance of humor and drama had not yet, according to an insider, been reached. Waxman and Williams began to butt heads with Steinman over the changes and other matters, namely the rate of speed at which the money was being raised. Steinman reportedly was behaving with such autocracy that he wanted Waxman and Williams removed from any association with the project.

Smelling trouble as he does, Michael Riedel scooped it in the *New York Post*, opening the article with: "*Dance of the Vampires* is making its way to Broadway but not without a splattering of bad blood." Riedel's assertion was not wrong nor was he mistaken about the fact that it seemed Waxman and Williams had been released from their obligations. Williams retorted: "There have been some disagreements, but every show has its bumpy road. This one may be having more bumps than others, but we are fully committed to it." She went on to say that: "We are prolific producers and we fully intend to continue our involvement in the show."

What Waxman and Williams appeared to not know at this point, however, was that Steinman had now tasked manager Sonenberg with steering the ship and that Steinman was effectively producing the show himself for the moment, a notion that Riedel pointed out was tantamount to "letting an inmate run the asylum."

Enter the former Phantom.

UK-born Michael Crawford had been a draw on the West End for years. On Broadway he achieved a certain legendary status for his tantalizing portrayal of the title role in Andrew Lloyd Webber's *The Phantom of the Opera*, winning the Tony Award for it. After the stint as the tormented Phantom ended in New York, Crawford accepted a sweetheart deal in Las Vegas doing a specialty show at a reported 20 million a year, but that came to an end prematurely after an injury sidelined him. All told, even though an impressive concert and recording career followed, in recent years Crawford's star has dimmed on both sides of the Atlantic and he was, well, "shopping" for a new musical. It could mean a "comeback" in that arena but perhaps all the better a fat payday every Thursday.

Getting Crawford entwined with the show that by now was stalled (would-be investors were vacillating in the aftermath of all the "who's the producer here" dramatics) would be a golden ticket. Crawford was looking for one himself. Under his terms, it was widely reported that Crawford would play a three-year stint in *Dance of the Vampires* (no one apparently paused to question whether the show would have that much staying power) and be granted the first rights of refusal to reprise the role in a film version (there were widespread rumors that Crawford was incensed when he was passed over for the film version of *The Phantom of the Opera*).

There was more. When an actor, no matter how considerable a drawing card they may be, demands "creative control" over their character, the wild horses have been let out of the barn. Writers and directors at this point have all but ceded their advantaged view from above, being thereby able to act in the best interest of the overall show.

Whether the folks at the top of the totem pole at *Dance of the Vampires* were naïve, dazzled, and humbled by Crawford's involvement, or just relieved to have a "name" onboard isn't known, but Crawford was signed to play the role of the vampire Krolock. It was a role that had been largely secondary in Europe but would now be beefed up and receive top billing for the New York outing. The price tag? A reported 30,000 dollars a week would go to Crawford. Steve Barton, the actor who had been "promised" the role for New York, was found dead the day after the announcement was made public that Crawford would play the role in what was rumored (although not substantiated) to be a suicide. Odds are that we'll never know whether Crawford's being hired impacted the tragedy.

Opening night on Broadway was set for April of 2002, but the September 11, 2001, terrorist attacks in the United States put a hold on that. As flyers were hesitant to travel internationally, logistics became problematic for the members of team *Vampires* based on opposite sides of the Atlantic. The opening date was pushed back to the fall of 2002. The show would miss the Tony Award cutoff deadline that season, but the postponement did mean that additional time was granted to raise production money, which apparently was still deficient.

There were other variables proving to impede the show's already well-strained migration to Broadway. One was psychology and the other was, to hear one production team member describe it, psychosis. It was believed by some involved that, market trend research notwithstanding, Broadway audiences post-9/11 were hungry for light, comedic fare, an argument more subjective than fact based but one that Crawford (remember that "creative control" clause in his contract) was seemingly obsessed with.

The draft of the "new" show that floated in late fall of 2001 apparently achieved more balance between the dramatic and the comedic, but Crawford began to have deep concerns that the role of Krolock was still reading too similar to that of the Phantom. One team member reported that "it was like he (Crawford) was 24/7 fixated, hell bent on staying as distant as possible from any comparisons (to the Phantom)."

Crawford didn't have to look far for allies and seemed to know that fresh talent coming onboard the team, particularly like-minded producers (of which there was still a dearth), would have his back. Housecleaning was imminent. Sonenberg as producer and Steinman as director were the first to go. Caird was reportedly bought out of his contract and the new producing team hit Steinman with a list of potential directors and choreographers for mulling over.

The design team from Europe was also out; suddenly the names of elite Broadway designers were finding their way onto company memos. Crawford was by now unapologetically and near autonomously rewriting the script, holding court with David Ives, who was still involved, explaining why what Ives had written wouldn't work. Not only did Crawford reportedly revise his character with the compulsion that Krolock must resemble the Phantom in no way or shape whatsoever, he also argued that Professor Abronsius, now the secondary male lead, should have no jokes of his own and should be relegated to the role of the "straight" man. Ives was befuddled and was heard to say of working with Crawford, "I'm not a writer—I'm a stenographer."

Crawford was also meddling in the matters of the costume design, insisting that his costumes be designed to conceal his body flab, particularly his droopy lower cheeks. Ruffled collars were put in place to conceal these, which by all accounts looked absurd. Mercifully these were cut by opening night, but not before cast members reportedly began to call Crawford a "Fat Rooster" when Crawford was out of earshot.

John Rando. Poor John Rando. The director of *Urinetown*, the hit satire musical that didn't close on Saturday night (in fact it had a hell of a good run despite the title), had the smarts aplenty. An amiable and diverse gentleman of the theatre, Rando essentially had the deck stacked against him from the genesis of his assignment as the new director of *Dance of the Vampires*, so he can hardly be blamed for inheriting the mess. To explain, and by way of a review, let's place some clear-eyed perspective on what Rando was dealing with even before he walked into the rehearsal room—a mess of a musical with an existential identity crisis that couldn't decide if it was a comedy or a melodrama with no less than a small army of producers, writers new and old, friends of those writers new and old, lawyers, managers, agents, designers, and others chiming in on what the show "should be" with hardly an agreement between them. And then there was Crawford asserting creative control over the direction of the script and, by insider accounts, behaving like a spoiled child.

Rando brought with him onto the production team his *Urinetown* choreographer John Caraffa, but behind the scenes many were whispering about this not having been a wise decision as Caraffa appeared to many to be generally out at sea, and this was hardly the time for that.

Nevertheless, Rando stayed the course and did what he could to salvage what he could into a comprehensible, linear story that somehow made sense, jived dramaturgically, and met the demands of a temperamental star. This was despite the temperamental star shutting the director down at nearly every turn or mere suggestion as to how to shape and refine the performance.

Finally, Steinman was fed up and had had enough with all the changes to the script and score which had become in his view too wild a departure from the European version. He stopped attending rehearsals after producers complained so loudly about his interruptions and "disruptive" behavior. Sonenberg was called to bring the hammer down on his own client and rein him in. Steinman knew the writing on the wall. He had provided the material that he was contractually obligated to provide and he was out.

And Kunze? The blood ran from his face when he finally caught wind of all the radical changes, seething silently at first but then wasting no time in contacting his lawyers. He was suing the Americans and wanted his name off the show, which at this point he didn't recognize as being the one he had written. Steinman reacted with a level head and asked Kunze to keep an open mind. Steinman invited Kunze to come to New York and see for himself. Maybe Kunze could be assuaged or, better yet, fall in line behind the production. Kunze wasn't in the mood for niceties. He was pressing ahead, lining up lawsuits.

And then a small miracle: Kunze's lawyers advised him to take a "wait and see" approach. Who knew if the show would be successful? Better to sit tight and not pour millions of dollars into a lawsuit that might destroy the show's chances of success, or so went the line of thinking. Kunze relented for the moment and accepted the invitation to New York. Once there, rather than finding the show-killing ogres that he had expected, Kunze was pleased to discover an army of talented and respectful actors, producers, and staff who welcomed his input, which Kunze didn't withhold. Irked by all the musical cuts to make room for what one person called a "fourth rate version of *The Producers*," Kunze encouraged restoring a good bit of it. He also dreamt up a new ending which ultimately fell on receptive ears.

Rando's mother had been unwell. With her death imminent Rando naturally took a leave of absence. Under a more "traditional" hierarchy of Broadway production personnel, at this stage an assistant director would run the day-to-day in place of the director. In certain instances, a choreographer might step up to the helm. It wouldn't be unheard of for a "stand-in" experienced director to, with certain understandings, take the place of the absentee director.

But none of these scenarios transpired. Rather, Michael Crawford insisted on assuming the role of the director during Rando's hiatus. There was little pushback. After all, Crawford did contractually have a certain degree of "creative control" and his star-power at the top of the marquee was the reason the show was selling well during previews. But many found it shocking, unorthodox, and even appalling to see and hear Crawford making daily changes and giving the rest of the cast notes on their performances. The asylum was indeed being run by the most feared inmate and no one was stopping it.

Crawford wasn't making many friends onstage either. He cut Professor Abronsius's (played here by Rene Auberjonois) laugh lines citing that it was critical that the role become the "straight man" in what was now, so Crawford thought, a riotous comedy. The two famously began a duel of purposely stepping on each other's lines onstage. Eventually many of the Professor's jokes were restored, but not without several hurricanes having run their course.

This was getting absurd. A press release revealed how far astray the musical had gone since leaving Germany (and how tacky, at that).

> MICHAEL CRAWFORD
> In
> *DANCE OF THE VAMPIRES*
> A new musical by Jim Steinman and Michael Kunze
> Based on the film by Roman Polanski
> Michael Crawford returns to Broadway for the first time since his Tony Award®-winning performance in *THE PHANTOM OF THE OPERA*. *DANCE OF THE VAMPIRES* is a hot-wired fairy tale in which an aristocratic, charismatic vampire, Count Von Krolock, jousts with a young passionate student, Alfred, to win the body and soul of a beautiful eighteen-year-old virgin, Sarah, who only knows that she wants . . . more!!!
> From an award-winning creative team comes the musical event of the season.
> *DANCE OF THE VAMPIRES* is a spectacular roller coaster ride, twisting and turning from romance to comedy to horror, all set against an opulent score and explosive dance.
> Get ready for a total eclipse over Broadway.

The perverse act of glee-taking in a show's misfortunes when reports from the inside are dismal brings out the flop musical buzzards. The reports from inside were indeed dismal. Broadway chat room boards lit up with reports of infighting, cast scandals, ticked off authors, and general unrest. As tends to happen, word on the street in the theatre community adopted the stance of judge, jury, and executioner even though many of them had not seen the show. Steinman would later remark that the show going on inside was a "runaway train" and that the show practically had a sign on its back that said "kick me!"

The opening night performance received a standing ovation, and to the surprise of many that evening and during the previews (and certainly despite the grief that the show had thus endured), audiences might, just might, be taking the bait. There were a great many scratching their heads. Crawford was, well, funny. Moreover, there were more than a few genuinely comedic moments that worked exceedingly well. The "Garlic" number appeared as hysterical satire and the first scene upstairs at the inn played like farce. Had the naysayers been wrong? And for the choreography, the same John Caraffa who had at first seemed at a loss as to how to make the show dance had turned out dancing that was sweepingly and uniformly gorgeous.

But fortitude of the comedy was compromised and shaken by what didn't quite fit. In a turn of the page, the show became sensual, dark, and brooding. Was this satire? Is this supposed to be funny? No one was certain. No. Yes. No. Huh? Moments later, the herky-jerkies returned as the show whipsawed into high comedy again. It felt like a theme park roller-coaster ride in the dark that lulls you into a false sense of security only to turn on a dime and zip you away into another dimension, taking your stomach with it.

All of this, to some extent, might have been excused as structural flaws. Many a musical has acquired an audience because of its merits and in spite of its flaws, structural or otherwise. But when Crawford and his would-be lady vampire took center stage and bellowed three minutes of "Total Eclipse of the Heart," the Steinman song made famous well before the fact by pop singer Bonnie Tyler, the show's fate was essentially sealed. This was simply inept theatre making of its own doing. But wait, an audience held its breath; this *is* supposed to be funny, right? And that, as described, encapsulates the better part of *Dance of the Vampires'* onstage experience.

So it's not surprising that the reviews were a mixed bag, leaving critics in a quandary as to whether to shoot down the show and dismiss it out of hand or applaud the parts that worked and leave it at that for an audience to decide for themselves.

"Goofy, off-the-wall fun," exclaimed the Associated Press review and many reviews lavished effusive praise on the cast, with CBS TV proclaiming that "Michael Crawford gives a powerhouse performance." Others were in the middle, not sure what to make of the whole state of affairs. Isherwood, in his review above, summed up the confusion amiably ("as a serious musical—well, it's pretty damn funny").

The dissenters, however, were more amplified:

> Oh Buffy, you Vampire Slayer—where were you when we needed you? There are altogether far too many vapid vampires in the new musical *Dance of the Vampires* which opened at the Miskoff Theatre last night. The necessary distinction between the undead and the unloving was never quite clear enough in this carelessly engineered (show) ....
>
> *Clive Barnes*, New York Post, *December 10, 2002*

Ken Mandelbaum buttoned it up thusly for *Broadway.com*:

> What no one involved seemed to realize was that the jokey new book would be at odds with the score, resulting in a show that doesn't seem to have a clue about what it wants to be ... Where Steve Barton's Vienna Krolock was allowed to be extravagant yet romantic, Crawford looks fairly ludicrous in his Liberace get-up. And because he's now "Count Giovanni von Krolock, from the Sicilian side of the family," he must also adopt a silly accent.

At this point, there was little to be done other than to wait, but the numbers at the box office began to slip precipitously and soon the advance ticket money had evaporated. A sixty-thousand-dollar-a-day take at the box office wasn't enough to cover the 600,000-dollar weekly operating cost. The producers christened a new advertising line for the show as "The One Broadway Musical That Really Sucks!" hoping to exact what they could from the comedy angle of marketing the show. Finally, they took a Hail Mary pass by allocating a few hundred thousand dollars for a television ad, but it didn't seem to help matters much. By January, all of the tourists were back at home. This was another rough break for the vampire show.

Steinman was incensed and embarrassed. His dreams of Broadway "cred" now thwarted; he went on the defensive with a steady drumbeat of denouncing the show and telling anyone who would listen that this mess was definitely and unequivocally not his fault or of his doing. And this ultimately proved to be the show's Broadway undoing. "The show that is dear to me is still running in Vienna. The one at the Minskoff was just a job," said Steinman publicly.

Finally, after 56 performances, *Dance of the Vampires* closed. At the time of closing, *Dance of the Vampires* was one of the most expensive failures in Broadway history losing a reported upwards of 12 million dollars. That dubious distinction was finally all but forgotten when previous expensive failures were all usurped by the closing of *Spider-Man: Turn Off the Dark*.

And we all know *that* story by now.